Travelling People

Victor Bewley

Travelling People

Veritas Publications Dublin 1974

First published 1974 by
Veritas Publications,
Pranstown House, Booterstown Avenue, Co. Dublin.

© 1974 Victor Bewley.

Printed and bound in the Republic of Ireland by
Cahill and Co. Limited, Dublin.

Designed by Liam Miller.
Cover by Steven Hope.

ISBN 0-901810-82-7.
CAT. NO. 3310,

Set in 10/11 Baskerville.
Cover photograph: Andrew McGlynn.

Contents

Preface

Ten years ago, if people thought of "the Itinerant problem" at all, they thought of it either as being a darned nuisance, a pollution of the countryside, a disgrace before tourists, a menace to property and person. Or else they thought of it as being a free and healthy way of life the itinerants themselves wanted. The *people* involved in this "problem" were rarely thought about at all, nor was anyone very concerned as to how this way of life affected them.

When the Government established the Commission on Itinerancy in 1960, many people were vaguely of the opinion that its purpose was to find ways and means of getting rid of the nuisance of itinerancy, or at least of sweeping it under the national carpet. In fairness to the minister responsible at the time, he did point out at the first meeting of the Commission that one of its responsibilities was to seek and find a way of life more in keeping with human dignity than that available to the Travellers at the time.

This Government Commission sat for three years. As Commissions go, it was very small, with only ten members. It is interesting to note, however, that more than ten years later the findings of the Commission are still regarded as being, in the main, very valid and very accurate. This, I would think, is due largely to the very wise decision of the Chairman, Mr Justice Brian Walshe, to go out and speak to the Travellers themselves and get to know their views—their real views—on the whole situation.

The Commission reported to the Government in 1963 and the Government accepted its report in October 1964. A year later nothing had happened, mainly because of the rather strong opposition of the

6

settled community. It was then that a group of people came together and established the *Dublin Itinerant Settlement Committee*. The original purpose of this committee was not to undertake settlement itself, but rather to seek ways and means to so change public opinion that it would be possible for Local Authorities to implement the new Government policy.

The first serious attempt at settlement was the provision of a trailer-caravan in a small unused part of a farmyard, offered to the Committee by Victor Bewley.

The Committee was so encouraged by the success of this initial venture that it began to look for similar small pieces of land in and around the city on which trailers and running water could be put, and in this way quite a number of families began on the path to settlement.

Thus the story began. This little book tells you how the story progressed. It cannot, however, tell you the ending. We cannot be certain that we are even on the right road. From the beginning the central theme of our policy has been quite clear, and contrary to the ideas of many people, it is not to persuade the Travellers to settle, or to settle them at any cost. We have always maintained, and still do, most strongly, that if the Travellers wish to continue travelling, then they have every right to do so, and it is the duty of society to allow them to do so in conditions that befit human dignity. On the other hand, if they wish to settle in our community, then we must accept them as we would any other neighbour. There may be a third option—they may decide to keep their own identity and accept as many of the benefits of settled living as appear good to them. This must be their decision: it is our privilege only to help them on that road.

THOMAS FEHILY
November 1974

Introduction

This book was written to give a brief outline of the position of the Travelling People in Ireland in the 1970s and to lay emphasis on the responsibility of Christians in this matter. It is not intended to be a full account of the history of the Travelling People and their way of life. I hope that some day this will be written by someone qualified to do so, perhaps by a Traveller.

Within the limitations of this book it has only been possible to indicate the sort of thing which is being done to meet the Travellers' needs at the present time. Perhaps one day a more detailed account may be written.

I would like to pay tribute to the work being done by many people, without whom the progress so far made would not have been possible. These include Government Ministers, T.D.s, members of local authorities, bishops, members of religious communities, clergy of different denominations, and many other devoted people.

1 The Travelling People in Ireland

It was March 1966. The day was bright and clear. There was a light breeze and the earth was damp after a shower of rain. As we stood on the Moor o' Meath a horse galloped past us, ridden by three young boys. Their faces were alight with excitement. As I watched them, I thought how much they had, compared with many boys who lived in more comfortable homes in the city. How much they would lose if they should ever change their way of life.

Their homes were nearby. One was a rather battered old motor caravan with a leaky roof, another a horse-drawn caravan and a third simply a canvas spread over bent sticks. The family slept on straw on the ground. Grim, I thought, in the winter; but the winter had passed and spring and summer lay ahead . . . . and the open road. I thought of the words:

Let other folk make money faster
in the air of dark-roomed towns,
I don't dread a peevish master
Though no man may heed my frowns.
I be free to go abroad,
Or take again my homeward road . . .
W. Barnes.

I had thought of these words, too, some twenty-five years earlier, when walking along a road near Caragh Lake in Kerry. A number of travelling families came towards us. They waved cheerfully as they passed on their little flat carts, piled high with an assortment of bundles. They looked happy and care-

11

free, living in the present, rather than worrying about the future. Were their lives more fully lived, more meaningful, than those of many a city dweller?

Twenty-five years earlier still we had lived on a small farm on the banks of the Dodder between Rathfarnham and Orwell Bridge. The gipsies, as we used to call them, would come and camp on the other side of the river, although we understood they were not allowed to stay there for more than three days. As a small boy I was fascinated by their gaily painted caravans and all the clutter of animals, bundles and children which they brought with them. I remember seeing them hunt their horses across the shallow river, to graze on our land. Of course, this did not please my father, but I was too young to worry about that, and used to dream of going to visit them. I wanted to get to know such interesting-looking people. Their life seemed so picturesque and romantic.

The next contact I had with the Travellers must have been about thirty years later. Walking along the road from Dingle to Castlegregory over the Connor Pass, I saw ahead of me by the side of the road a small brown tent. Smoke drifted up from a fire, beside which were a man and some childen. As I approached, the man moved slightly forward, as though he might have been going to say something. We exchanged good evenings, but he didn't say any more, which wasn't surprising, as I never slackened my pace, but kept steadily walking on. Many years later, looking back, I still feel that man would have said more, had I given him the chance. Why didn't I stop? Was he not one of the people that had so fascinated me in earlier life? What had happened since? Two things perhaps. There was nothing picturesque or romantic about this man and his simple camp. On the contrary he was shabby and down-trodden in appearance, with rather a hopeless expression on his face. For my part,

I had been conditioned by all that had happened since childhood.

The strange, rather wild appearance of the man repelled rather than attracted me as though I was pervaded with a vague fear, which puts us on our guard when we meet the unusual or unknown. Perhaps too I had a feeling that he was going to ask for something, and even if I gave him something, he would still ask for more. Without realising it, a barrier had arisen between me and the Travellers of the road. I was a member of the settled community and these people were somehow outside and apart, and to be regarded with reserve, if not suspicion. Reflecting on such moments we can see something of the meaning of the words of Jesus: "Unless you change and become like little children, you will never enter the kingdom of heaven" (Mt 18:3). What a pity that as we grow up we often lose the open mind of a child, who simply sees another human being, unfettered by fears and prejudices which may warp our lives and cloud our vision in later years, thus losing that spirit which helps us to see all men as brothers.

In the winter of 1964 there were a number of articles in the papers referring to the Travelling People. They had gathered in increasing numbers around Dublin, and antagonism was rising against them. A number of families were camped at Inchicore, and I passed them daily on my way to work. One morning the caravans were all out in a line on the road. The guards were there. The families were being moved from their camping place. When they had left, the entrance to the ground was blocked so that they could not return. This was to happen many times, in many places.

Most of us had assumed that these people were happy in their way of life, and had no wish to settle down, yet the very fact that they had to be compelled to move seemed to contradict this. If these people did

want to settle should they not be given somewhere to
do so? Was it right that they should be forcibly kept
on the move? Could we really go on doing this to our
fellow Irish men and women?

I could not help feeling increasingly uneasy, and
hoped someone would do something about it. Like
most other people I felt this wasn't my problem—or
was it? Are we not all part of the community in which
we live, and have a share in the responsibility for what
goes on particularly if we are aware of injustice, yet
do nothing about it? We all have a voice. We can all
speak to someone. If we remain silent when we should
speak, we share in the common guilt. "Everyone who
knows what is the right thing to do and doesn't do it,
commits a sin" *(Jm 4:17)*.

In December 1965 I was in London on business.
Having heard that a camping site had been provided
in Hertfordshire for some gipsy families who wanted
to settle down, I went to see it. There were five
families living there. They each had hard standing
for their caravan, and a wooden chalet which was
used as a living room. There was water and sanitation. I asked one of the mothers if she did not miss
moving around as they had done in the past. "No,"
she said, "life on the road is over. Our children must
get education if they are to make a living in the
future." I asked her if she would like to live in a
house. She said she wouldn't. She had tried it, but
felt the walls were coming in on top of her. The
arrangements on the camp site suited her very well,
as she was in and out of the fresh air all the time,
and this was what she was used to. However, she
hoped that her children would get used to being in
buildings while at school, and would eventually become part of the settled community. Later I was to
hear the same sentiments expressed many times by
Irish Travellers.

Origin of the travelling people

Little is known about the origin of the Travellers. The report of the Government Commission makes the following observations: "Itinerants who were questioned on this subject could furnish little or no information and, indeed, displayed remarkably little interest in their origins. They did not appear to have any folklore on the subject . . . Few of the itinerants in Ireland are of Romany or Gipsy origin . . . The list of surnames recorded in the census taken for the Commission discloses that almost all itinerants in the country bear Irish surnames. . . .

"The existence of itinerants in Ireland has been ascribed to many causes. It is said that they are descendants of the remnants of Irish tribes dispossessed in the various plantations. Some are said to be the descendants of the journeying craftsmen and metal workers who travelled the country centuries ago. Others are said to be the descendants of those who were driven to a wandering way of life because of the poverty and distress caused by the famines of the last century, the oppressions of the penal law era and earlier. It is likely that a combination of all these factors to a greater or lesser degree was responsible for the greater number of those now on the road."

In the past they were horse dealers, tinsmiths and travelling salesmen. Many people will remember seeing the little flat carts going around the country with rolls of linoleum, etc., for sale. These may still be seen in some places. Many people, too, will remember the tinsmiths who came round selling and repairing buckets, milkcans and other utensils. This was how they got the name Tinker, but now this has become a derogatory word and they dislike it. They were a respected people then, performing a useful service. They often brought news from one place to another, before the days of wireless and newspapers.

As the years went by, times changed. Horses became less in use, although there are still a number of
horse dealers, but the travelling salesmen and the
tinsmiths are no longer needed. With their means of
livelihood going, like other country people they began to drift to the cities and towns in order to make
a living. They came to the city ill-equipped for city
life. Most of them were illiterate, only about 10 per
cent could read and write. When they camped in
numbers together, their sites soon became dirty,
having no water and no sanitation. Many had to beg
for a living and this habit, together with their wandering horses, all helped to build up opposition to
them from the settled community.

In 1960, the Government appointed the Commission on Itinerancy to see what was the best way to
help these people. In 1963 the Commission produced
a most interesting report. Since then they have been
called Itinerants, to avoid using the word Tinker.
However, this is rather a clumsy word and they refer
to themselves as Travellers.

The Commission's report says that in 1961 there
were 1,100 Travelling families in the Republic. This
made a total of about 6,000 people. Over 900 families,
when asked, said that they would like to settle down.
Numerically, therefore, it is not a big problem. It is
only difficult of solution because of its nature. The
greatest injustice which was done to the Travellers
was that there was nowhere that they were legally
entitled to stay without fear of eviction. This was one
of the reasons why so few of them had had any
education.

The Commission's report recommended ". . . that
the provision of approved camping sites should be
undertaken where numbers of itinerant families
habitually frequent an area and where the immediate
provision of dwellings presents difficulties or where it
is clear that a majority of the itinerant families in

the areas would not at present accept houses. . . .
Local authorities should be required as soon as possible to ascertain the number of families regularly in
their areas and decide whether they are in a position
to consider them for housing within a short period. If
not, they should make immediate arrangements to
provide camping sites."

In 1964 the Minister for Local Government asked
the local authorities throughout the country to provide these sites and offered financial assistance. By
1965, however, nothing had been done. The reason
for this was that whenever it was proposed by any
local authority to provide a site it was always so bitterly opposed by those in the neighbourhood that in
the end the project was abandoned.

The Commission's report states that "it will be
vitally necessary for the success of any scheme for the
absorption and rehabilitation of itinerants to have in
each area in which it is proposed to settle a number
of itinerant families local voluntary committees . . .
who are prepared to interest themselves directly in
the settlement of the families concerned. The main
purpose of such committees would be to bridge the
gap between the itinerant family and the settled
community."

Early in 1965 the Dublin Itinerant Settlement
Committee was formed with this purpose in mind,
and to try to win the support of public opinion for
having camping sites provided. Gradually committees
were formed in other places, and in 1969 the Irish
Council for Itinerant Settlement was formed to act as
a coordinating link between the various Committees.
In 1974 there are now committees in most of the
thirty-two counties. Rev. G. T. Fehily is Chairman of
the Council. In 1973 the name of the Council was
changed to The National Council for Travelling
People.

The present position

As any attempt by the local authority to provide a site was so bitterly opposed, in 1965 the Dublin Committee decided to start themselves to settle families on privately owned ground, and six motor caravans were bought for this purpose. At first it proved impossible to get any ground on which to place the caravans, but gradually small sites were made available and the first family moved into their new home at the end of December 1965. On the day they moved in, the first thing the mother of the family remarked on was the supply of water which was available. Often they had had to beg for water in the past.

They were very happy for a couple of weeks, but then as the novelty wore off they began to feel lonely. The site was very isolated. They were part of a large group of families and they began to miss the company of their relatives and friends. At the end of another week on a dark afternoon as the snow was falling, they left their new home to return to join their relatives on the road.

A couple of years later, the same family was offered a corporation house, and moved into it with great joy. They were welcomed by the neighbours. Again, all went well for a while, but later they once more longed for the company of the family circle. They could not keep scrap in their new house, and this was a big disadvantage as it was their means of livelihood. After three months, they once more returned to the road. This time the father said: "I see now what I really want is a camping site, where I can stay with my own people and follow my own way of life." Some time later he had the opportunity to move on to such a site and is still there.

The next three families were found a place to settle early in 1966. Six years later they moved into County Council houses, where they are now happily

settled. Another family which moved onto a single
site in 1966 lived there for two years, but finally felt
too lonely and left to join some of their relatives on
a larger site which had been opened later. However,
an old feud existed between them and another family
on the same site, and finally because of this they left
and returned to the road.

These few incidents must be typical of experience
in many places. Isolated sites on the whole are not
suitable. Some families like to be on their own or
with one other family on a small site, while others
like to be with a large number of families. Some
would like houses and would make a success of them,
while others do not want this or are not ready for it
at present. It is necessary therefore to study the
family and ascertain their wishes, and then help them
to get the type of accommodation which is appropriate to their need.

In 1967 Dublin Corporation opened their first
camping site for Travellers. It is called Labré Park
and has accommodation for thirty-nine families. A
second site, Avila Park, was opened in 1969 with
accommodation for twenty families. Each family is
provided with a place to park their caravan and tigin
(prefabricated chalet) consisting of a living room with
a solid fuel stove for heat and cooking, a toilet, sink
and tap. There is also a place to keep scrap as the
majority of families collect it. When these sites were
planned it was envisaged that the tigin would serve
as additional accommodation to the caravan, but, in
fact, most families moved into the tigin and used it
virtually as a house, for which, of course, it was not
designed and was inadequate. After some time a number of families on both sites asked if another room
could be added to the tigin. This indicated that the
families were settling more quickly and completely
than was expected. When the third site, Cara Park,
was planned each family was provided with a chalet,

consisting of a living room, three bedrooms and a bathroom and toilet. This site was opened in 1973 and caters for thirty-five families. The National Council for Travelling People has recommended that in future all chalets should provide three bedrooms.

As well as the three large sites in Dublin, there are a number of small sites accommodating one, two or more families. A few families have moved into houses, but the majority of those in Dublin at present would not want to move into a corporation or council house as they would have nowhere to keep their scrap by which they live. Psychologically also a large housing estate is unsuitable for most of them, as many would tend to feel isolated in it and to miss the company of their friends. It seems therefore that movement into houses in Dublin will be slow, although this may change with the next generation.

The position varies throughout the country. Nowhere is there as large a concentration of Travellers as around Dublin. Dundalk has a site for twenty-two families but very few other places will require a site of this size. In Shinrone, Offaly, there is a site for twelve families and several other counties have sites for smaller numbers. In some places, such as Cork, Kilkenny and Tuam, a number of families have moved into houses. Kerry County Council have an interesting plan which is to provide small camping sites for one or two families in different places and later to build cottages on them. At present forty of the fifty-six families which normally live in Kerry have been provided with such sites and some of the cottages have already been built.

This scheme has a great deal to commend it as the camping sites, and later the cottages, can often be located in the areas where the families have camped in the past. As they have a small plot of ground, they can continue to keep a horse and collect scrap if they so wish. Their pattern of life is not interrupted, but the door is open to them to move towards a settled life, and become integrated with the settled population. If this scheme were too rigidly implemented, it might have the effect of breaking up family groups and this would be a pity.

The Travellers as a whole are not a community, but their loyalty is to their own family group. These ties are very strong and should be preserved. They have considerable social advantages. When the mother of a family has to go to hospital, there is someone to care for the children, if she is living near some of her relatives. When the parents get old, there is someone at hand to care for them, if their married sons or daughters are nearby. These family relationships are being lost in settled life in large towns at the present time. How many isolated families and lonely individuals in cities at present would welcome the feeling of belonging to a family circle? Of course, not all members of all families get on with each other or want to live together, but where they do, the relationship should not be cut across by "copybook rules".

In a country which rightly values the importance of family life, it is astonishing how often well-intentioned people propose to disrupt it. Again it must be stressed that the Travellers' own wishes should be found out and conditions provided in accordance with them insofar as is possible. The same remarks apply to our whole approach to the Travellers. Life should be given an opportunity to grow and develop creatively rather than be forced into a preconceived pattern.

In the last eight years more than seven hundred families have been provided with a place in which to live, at least to the extent that they need no longer fear eviction. Many, however, are living in conditions which are inadequate and were only intended for temporary use. Progress must be continued until all families have adequate accommodation. There are probably still about five hundred or more families on the road, who would like a place in which to settle. In 1961 the Government Commission found on enquiry that there were less than 200 families that wished to continue to travel. The same is probably still true today.

The Commission recommended that properly equipped halts should be provided for such families in different places so that when they camped, they would have the facilities of water and sanitation in the same way that camping sites are provided for holiday-makers on the continent at present. There is a group of families who visit Dublin from time to time dealing in antiques and other things. They show no desire to settle, but would appreciate a proper place in which to camp when they come to Dublin, and would be willing to pay for it. At present, however, there is no such place available for them.

Education

As more families settle, more of their children are able to attend school. Just as plans for settlement must vary with local needs and conditions so must the plans for education. Few of the children can go straight into the normal classes and take their proper place in them. Many of them are already past the usual age for starting school. They are not used to sitting down and concentrating for long periods. They are not used to being in buildings or taking instructions from other people.

A time of preparation is therefore necessary before they can join a normal class and benefit by it. We have found in some places that Travelling children have been placed in normal schools without adequate preparation. Although their attendance is recorded, they are unable to benefit by the education, and may well come out of school illiterate. Teachers with large classes are unable to give the necessary individual attention which such children need and this should be provided beforehand.

Hundreds of Travelling children are now getting education in a variety of ways. Only time will tell which arrangement is the most beneficial. The one tried at Finglas in Dublin by the Sisters of the Holy Faith has much to commend it. When the site in Finglas first started, forty-five children from it were admitted to two special classes in the nearby national school. At first they went for two hours a day, but this time was gradually lengthened until by the end of the school year, they were having normal school hours. They had a 95 per cent attendance for the year. The second year the girls were all transferred to the normal classes. The boys could not be transferred in this way, as it was a girls' school. The boys might have been transferred to the local boys' school, but this would have cut across the relationship which Sister de la Salle, the principal of the school, had established with them, and which had proved so valuable. The boys continued therefore in their special class for another year, but at the end of that time were successfully transferred to the boys' school, so that all the children are now integrated in normal classes.

A friendly, understanding, personal relationship is of great importance. This can often prove most valuable in the time of preparation, and encourages attendance at school. This may be interrupted at the time of transfer to normal classes and attendance is sometimes found to suffer. A member of a voluntary committee can sometimes help here by sympathetic understanding and encouraging attendance.

The importance of proper preparation for school is illustrated by the case of two little boys who started off at the local national school. As well as being unable to keep pace with their classmates, in various other ways they did not fit in. They had lived in very primitive conditions in the past and were not used to using toilets as they had never had anything but the hedges. This proved a difficulty at school and only made them conspicuous. The teacher asked that they be removed from the school as they were not benefiting by being there. They then went for a while to a special school for Travelling children under the care of the kindly Sister Albertus, of the Sisters of Charity. There they received the special help which they needed.

Later they returned to the national school and this time fitted in satisfactorily. The living conditions of the family have considerable bearing on attendance at school. One family of children, who after preparation had been admitted to a national school, had to leave again as they were unable to keep up the necessary standard of health and hygiene, due to their appalling living conditions.

Families who are forced to keep moving from place to place are unable to send their children to school, unless arrangements are made by a voluntary committee to collect the children by bus and bring them to school. It was such conditions that led to the starting of St Kieran's School in Bray. This school and the whole subject of education of Travellers is discussed more fully in a later chapter.

Occupation

The majority of families collect scrap either by horse and cart, or by van. When they can afford a van they can cover a greater area and make a better living. Scrap collecting is often objected to by the settled population, because the scrap looks so unsightly when kept at the side of the road. We should remember, however, that the Travellers do not make the scrap. The scrap is what the settled population no longer want. The Travellers perform a useful service in taking it away. It is a respectable occupation. It does look unsightly at the side of the road, but that is not the fault of the Travellers, it is the fault of the settled community who have failed to give the Travellers a proper place in which to live where they could also keep their scrap. Some families collect rags also. Others lay tarmacadam and this can be a profitable occupation. Antique dealing is becoming increasingly popular and can yield a good living also. All these occupations suit the Travellers as they do not involve working to routine, but can be done in their own time.

In the country many families will do casual work on farms, but of course this is only seasonal work. An increasing number are going into regular employment. A few years ago there were hardly any Travellers in employment in Dublin. Now there are over thirty. The same pattern is found in a number of other places. As most of the adults at present are illiterate, they can only get unskilled jobs, but when the children who are at present at school start to look for work, many more doors will be open to them. No one knows how deep the urge to travel goes, but if one has education, there are a number of interesting ways in which one can satisfy this urge, which are not open to those who are illiterate.

Opposition by the settled community

Nine years ago, as we started to help the first families to find a place to settle, people said to us: "When the first bird sings in the spring, they'll be off down the road. They don't want to settle." "They'll never send their children to school, they are not interested in education." "They won't work, they are too lazy." "Do you really think you'll get their coopera-

tion?" In those days we could only answer these
questions by saying what we thought were the answers.
Now there is the evidence of what is actually the
case, as has been described in the foregoing pages.

It is no longer in doubt that the majority do want
to settle, will send their children to school, and are
prepared to earn their living. There is now no reason
for denying them these opportunities on the grounds
that they don't want them. There is no financial
reason for denying them these opportunities either,
for the Government announced in the Spring Budget,
1970, that the State would pay the full cost of providing suitable accommodation for Travelling
families who want to settle. Why then is this not done
without further delay? Because of apathy and opposition. Apathy on the part of many of the settled population and some local authorities, because they do not
realise how some of our fellow Irishmen are being
treated. They don't know, and often don't want to
know. Opposition by the residents, which usually
arises in any area in which a local authority proposes
to provide accommodation for Travellers. There are,
of course, exceptions, but unfortunately they are still
exceptions. One of the most heartening of these was
the West Finglas Tenants' Association.

About eighteen Travelling families had been
camped in Finglas for some months, close to the
houses. The site was dirty, insanitary, and rat in-
fested. While the residents naturally complained
about this state of affairs, they also said that they
were willing for the families to remain in the area, if
they were properly accommodated. One could wish
that such an enlightened and Christian attitude
would prevail more often, and then local authorities
would be ready to provide the necessary accommodation. As a result, everyone would be better off,
Travellers and settled community alike. It is not in

anyone's interest to have the Travellers treated as many are at present. It would be in everyone's interest to have them properly provided for.

What is the basis for the opposition? The root of it is, I think, fear. Fear of the unknown. Fear of people who look different. Fear that their camping sites will become unsightly and insanitary, causing a health hazard. Fear of nuisance caused by begging, wandering horses and dishonesty. Fear that these people will do what they like, and never cooperate or accept the standards which most of us have to accept in order to live together in a congenial community. Fear that property will be devalued. There is, of course, a basis for all these fears. All these things happen, except perhaps the last. We make a mistake, however, when we think that all Travellers are like that or want to be like that. Many of these nuisances arise, not from the people themselves, but from the conditions in which they have to live. Many of them will change when the conditions change. This has been proved over and over again.

There is nothing to fear about the Travellers. Most of them are friendly, warm-hearted people. There are, of course, some troublesome individuals such as you would find in any community. Many of their present camping sites are, of course, dirty and insanitary. It is impossible for them to be otherwise under the conditions in which they have to live. No water, no sanitation, muddy ground. This is the advantage to the settled community of a properly-equipped site, it gets rid of this objectionable aspect and is, of course, of the greatest benefit to the Travellers. Constant begging is, naturally, objected to, but as things are at present, many families have little alternative but to beg. Wandering horses are a great nuisance and often a great danger. As long as the people have to wander, so will the horses. As the people settle, the number of horses tends to diminish and some families are renting grazing for their animals, though they often find this difficult to get.

Of course, some Travellers are dishonest, just as some settled people are dishonest. We must not judge the majority by the few. When treated reasonably, they are just as well able to and as likely to cooperate as anyone else. When they are treated as outcasts, why should they cooperate or consider the wishes of those who have had so much greater opportunities in life, yet reject them? There is no reason why a properly-equipped camping site should cause the devaluation of neighbouring property. Even if it did, should not the needs of human beings come before the value of property? Unfortunately, it is a sad reflection on our social thinking today that too often property is considered before men, women and children. Is there not a real danger that the more affluent we become, the more materialistic we become? "Do not store up treasures for yourself on earth. . . . For where your treasure is, there will your heart be also" *(Mk 6:19-21).*

If we read in our newspapers an account of people being treated in some other country, in the way that Irish Travellers are treated in Ireland in the 1970s, we would be horrified and full of righteous indignation. A few examples will illustrate this.

A family camped by the roadside were woken early on Christmas morning and told to move. They asked if they could have breakfast first. They were not allowed to. The mother asked where they could go. The men who were moving them replied: "Get to hell out of that." She answered: "We wouldn't be welcome in hell from this Christian country."

A group of families camping in their usual place were joined by some others. It was a thinly-populated area, but some of the local residents gathered a crowd from a wide area which descended on the Travellers and ordered them to move. Two of their tents were demolished and thrown on the road. These tents were the only homes these people had. They left quietly simply because they were afraid to stay, as the guards had told them they could not offer them any protection if they did.

When we visited them after this, they were very frightened and said to us: "We don't know how long we shall be left there. Where can we go if we are moved, and who will offer us any protection?" We could not answer these questions; nor could anyone else. There was, in fact, nowhere that they could go and have any legal right to be here. Yet they were not strangers. They had lived all their lives around this particular town. One mother said: "I want my children to have what I never had—education." A father said : "I want my children to settle down, to join the settled people and forget about the road." It was a dreadful thing to listen to these people, and to realise that legally they were not entitled to be anywhere. What a betrayal of the ideals of our country . . . "to cherish all the children. of the nation equally". What a betrayal of our Christian faith! What a scandalous denial of all that Jesus taught us! What rank hypocrisy to pretend to give allegiance to that faith, and to treat our fellow men in this way! "This is my commandment: love one another as I have loved you" (*Jn 15:12*).

After a meeting in another town, at which Fr Fehily and I had spoken, a number of people came to speak to us. The first was a leading citizen of that town. He said: "Of course there is no problem with the Travellers here. They come for a while, but they never seem to want to stay. They always go again." The next person who came was a nun from the Convent of Mercy. She said that from time to time they had children of Travellers in their school. "But," she said, "it's most frustrating." "What is frustrating?" I asked. "Aren't the children good at their work?" "Oh, yes," she said, "that's just the point. They are, and

just when they're settling down and making progress,
they're moved." "Who moves them?" I asked. "Is it
the local authority?" "Oh no," she said, "they just do
nothing. It's the local residents that move them."

In another town we met a widow with nine
children. Four of them had been attending school,
but this was interrupted when the family was moved
from their camping place. In the same town we
visited ten families camped along the side of a quiet
by-road. It was a dark morning, with the rain falling
steadily. There were pools of water in many places,
and the ground was soft and muddy. Some of the
people were lighting fires under covers of sacking to
shelter them from the rain. It seemed appalling to
think of people living like that, when there was
plenty of land in the area on which they could have
lived and the State would bear the cost of providing
accommodation for them. One might well have asked
why on earth this had not been done. How could the
local authority be so indifferent as to leave them
there? How inhumanly callous the residents must be
not to demand that the local authority make provision for them immediately. Did they do this? Not
likely!

As if this wasn't bad enough, six of these
families had been brought to court the previous week
for causing an obstruction on the road! If they had
not left this road within a month they would be
brought to court again and fined! If under our legal
system a fine is considered an appropriate penalty for
these people for causing some obstruction on this
little-used road, what would be an adequate penalty
for a local authority and a community which treated
its fellow men in this way? This was not in some
other country. This was how Irish people treated
other Irish people in the autumn of 1970.

"In so far as you did this to one of the least of
these brothers of mine, you did it to me" (Mt 25:40).

Do we understand?

How often do we blame other people for being what they are, without having any understanding of what has made them so? How often do we see the faults in others, rather than their better qualities, and by dwelling on their faults, accentuate them? Due to our clumsy negative approach, we are unaware of the sensitive feelings which are reaching out for something higher and better in life, and hinder, rather than encourage development.

The following incidents have taught me much, and I record them in case they are of interest to others.

Do not crush what is good

A young mother was about to go into hospital to have her eighth baby. As the family were camped on their own, I asked the father who would mind the children while the mother was away, as he was out all day at work. "Oh," he said, "they'll be all right." The eldest was a girl of twelve, and the youngest was a year old. While the mother was in hospital I went twice to visit them. Everything seemed to be going well. The eldest girl was washing the baby, while another was on her knees washing out the caravan. They were as cheerful as ever.

While I was there, the younger ones stood round me and held my hands. In the little squeezes of their hands, I felt I sensed that underneath they missed their mother, and were glad to see an older familiar person. Otherwise all was as usual. As I stood looking at them I wondered how many families in the settled population could carry on like that if the mother was away. I realised how these children were being prepared to meet life as they would find it, and how sensitive one should be so as not to crush their independent spirit.

Begging

She stood in Grafton Street frequently, with two small children beside her, and her baby in her arms. Today it was raining and the baby was under her coat. As I passed, she smiled down at her. The little face burst into smiles in return. She bent her head and kissed the little mite. She was no longer a pathetic-looking beggar. She was a mother, loving her baby, just like any other mother. Standing there begging, she was following the way of life she had been born to, just as her mother and grandmother had done before her. Perhaps one day her baby would do the same, or would she? Would some other door in life open to her, so that she would have no need to beg?

Another day I was standing waiting for someone in the street. Suddenly, I heard people speak to me and I was surrounded by four young girls and a boy, out begging. They were the aggressive type. They got a real kick out of watching people coming along the street, and trying to see how much they could extract from them. They could be pleading, or aggressive and abusive, according to which they thought would be most effective. They turned their charm on me, but soon stopped when they found it was of no avail, and we chatted normally. They asked if I would get them a job. What an asset their vitality and cheerfulness would be in a job, but how much preparation they would need! So far, life had given them no opportunity to go to school. Life had been primitive and hard for them, but it hadn't got them down. God love them.

A friend of mine told me that one wet day she passed a caravan and felt so sorry for the people in it in such wild weather. She went home and made some soup and brought it back to the caravan. It was, of course, welcomed, but immediately the mother produced a list of further needs—milk for the baby, and could she spare a little tea and sugar, etc.? My friend went home discouraged, just as many others have felt discouraged by similar approaches.

A few years ago the Dublin Committee was offered twenty mattresses by a boarding school, for distribution to the Travellers. As I was thanking the kind donor, my thought wandered from mattresses to blankets. We wanted blankets very much, and at the time had no funds to buy them. I was about to say "You wouldn't have any blankets to spare, would you?" but felt how ungrateful this would sound when we had just been given twenty mattresses. I realised in that moment how many a Travelling woman must feel when she thinks she has a sympathetic listener.

Someone said to me once: "I get the impression that you are against begging?" I said: "I certainly am, I think it's degrading." However, we can't just stop it abruptly, much as we may want to. We must allow time for life to change. A member of one committee told me that when they had found a place for the first two families to settle in their district, they forbade them to beg. After a while, they realised that this meant that the mothers never met anyone. They felt confined at home all day, whereas before they were out on their rounds, and as well as collecting money and clothes, etc., they were making contacts, often friendly contacts with other people. Many people have made friendly contacts with those who call at their doors by offering them something to eat or drink, and this is of great value.

It is easier to give to those who beg, than to refuse. If we give money we may be helping to perpetuate begging. It can be very profitable in some places. If we give money it may ease our conscience and we may do nothing about changing the conditions which make people beg. The latter is the more important.

B

Animals

Wandering horses and aggressive begging are
understandably two of the things which most turn
people against the Travellers. In more than one case
I have known of committees who insisted that the
Travellers got rid of their horses when they settled
down. It proved to be a mistake. The men had then
nothing to occupy them, no means of collecting
scrap. Financially, they were no worse off. They were
getting help from the State, supplemented by charity,
but they had lost their independence and initiative
and degenerated.

Drinking increased with idleness and boredom.
We should not cut across their way of life in this way,
but rather open up opportunities for life to grow in
other directions. As they settle, some provision should
be made for their animals also, if they have them.

A young woman who had settled down with her
own family asked me if I would go and visit her
parents, as they would like to find a place on which
to settle. We went to see them. They had three
horses; two belonged to a son who lived with them,
and one belonged to the old man. The son said he
would sell his horses if he settled, as he would not
need them. The daughter gave her old father a great
lecture on all the things he would have to do if he
settled down, including selling his horse. I don't
know what made her say that, as I had not mentioned
it. The old man listened very patiently, without saying a word, and when she had finished, he turned to
me and said: "I have had my pony since she was a
foal. I couldn't possibly part with her." One could
feel here the tremendous tie between these people
and their animals, and this must be borne in mind
when helping them to settle down.

One day we went to see an old man and his wife,
who were thinking of settling down. As we drew up,

they were squatting by their fire in front of a small tent. As the car stopped they made no move to greet us, but sat there glowering, their two dogs, which were tied up, barking furiously. As we got out of the car they smiled, and came to welcome us: "Ah," they said, "sure we thought you were tinkers!" They explained that there was another family camped in a lane nearby, but they were a "rough class of people," and they wouldn't have anything to do with the likes of them. One often finds that the quieter families wish to avoid those who they feel may be noisy or troublesome. This old pair had had one son, who ran away when he was fourteen. He would be twenty-one now. They were always hoping to find him as they wandered the roads.

All the time we talked, the two dogs kept barking. They explained that one of the dogs was vicious, and bit everyone except the old lady. I pointed out that if they settled down, they would be living beside other people with children and they would really have to get rid of the dog that bit. The old man said that would be all right, and I thought he was quite pleased with the idea. However, the old lady was quiet for a moment, and then said: "We got this dog as a pup, the week my son ran away. I couldn't let him go." The dog had somehow taken the place of her son. They decided to travel a little longer. I looked at their few possessions and wondered was there a lesson for us. Do we in our affluent society possess our possessions? Or do our possessions possess us? If they possess a man, "the worries of this world and the lure of riches choke the word and so he produces nothing" (Mt 13:22). Do they hinder our lives, and warp our sense of values?

On another occasion we were told of a family who were being moved from their camping-place and wanted to know where they could settle. We were horrified to see their conditions. Bits of old canvas, carpets and scrap were thrown over bent sticks and this was the home of a mother, two girls and a boy. The mother and girls welcomed us, but the boy remained surly in the background. He obviously considered us intruders and wished to have nothing to do with us, so we left him alone. The mother explained that he was very troublesome, and would often throw stones at her. A few days later I went again to see them, and this time took a photograph of the tent. The boy remained aloof as on the previous occasion. The mother asked me if I would photograph their three hens. I said: "Yes, of course. Do they lay any eggs for you?" "Not at all," she said. "We only keep them for company!" As I went to photograph the hens the boy got up and came with me. They were obviously his pets.

When that was done, he said: "Will you photograph the dog?" "Yes," I said, "would you like to be photographed with him?" "I would," he said. We were friends now. When they moved to their new home in a caravan, the children went to school, and the boy was able to play football with the other boys, thus giving him an outlet for his energy. The shade for one of the gas lights had a hole in it, so on my next visit I brought a replacement with me. While I was clumsily trying to fix the small shade, the boy said: "Shall I do it for you?" In a few moments his nimble fingers had done the job. As I looked at his beaming face, I felt what a change had come in this friendly, helpful boy from the day we first made friends through the animals. He seemed to me to be at the crossroads. So little could push him one way or the other now. Would he grow up surly and anti-social, or friendly and helpful?

Drink

It is a great mistake to assume that all Travellers

drink to excess. They do not. There are, of course, those for whom drink is a problem, just as there are those in the settled community for whom drink is a problem, but this does not mean that this is true for all Travellers or all of the settled community. There are some who drink just because they have nothing else to do, and it has been noticed that as they develop other interests, drinking decreases. We should try to understand, rather than to condemn.

Some years ago, anyone passing through Milltown one evening would have seen a little party of travelling men and women, sitting by the side of the road drinking. They had obviously been doing this for some time. I am sure that many who passed by made harsh judgments on them, but very, very few knew the tragedy that lay behind this scene. It was November. These two families had recently moved into Milltown, with very poor tents. One of them had a nine weeks old baby. One day the mother was going to the convent of the Sisters of Charity to get some medicine. She had her baby with her, and went into a shop on the way. The shopkeeper noticed that there was something wrong with the baby. It was dead. It had died in its mother's arms. This was such a shock to the poor mother that she was unable to speak and had to go into hospital. This left the father with six children, and their only means of support was the children's allowance.

The young man and his wife living next to them had two children, and they had absolutely nothing to live on except begging. They asked if we could move them into caravans to get them off the ground for the winter. This was done. At the end of a week we went to see them. They weren't sure that they were going to be able to settle. The site was rather isolated and lonely. There were very few people about and no lights at night. Although they had always travelled, they had camped on the outskirts of a town or village, where there were people about and lights at night. They said they would like to try a little longer. We went to see them again at the end of a second week. By this time, the mother was out of hospital, and nothing would do her, but she must go at once. She said she couldn't possibly live here, the place would get on her nerves. As we had no other site, we had to do as they asked, and agreed to move them back to Milltown with their tents the next day. The father followed us to the gate of the field. He said: "I am very disappointed. I was just beginning to settle myself; but it's no good; my wife is cursing me every day. We must go." We moved them the following day.

A fortnight later they came back to us. They had been flooded out in their tents, and asked if they could go back to the caravans they had left. But it was too late. We had no caravans and no sites left. This was on a Tuesday. On Thursday the baby in the second family had died of pneumonia. These two deaths occurred on the doorstep of our capital city, with all our modern conveniences for keeping ourselves dry and warm in the winter. Without trying to be sensational or dramatic, we must make it known that this is what is happening. This state of affairs cannot go on. Proper provision must be made for these people.

Another family, whom we were asked to help, were living in deplorable conditions when we found them. The father appeared to make no effort to help himself. He seemed content to let his wife and children go out begging, and he would drink the money when they came home with it. If you put him in touch with a job, he probably wouldn't go. If he did, he would only stay a couple of days, and then wouldn't come home until all his money was gone. It seemed impossible to make any progress. About a year later he made a great effort. He got a job him-

self. The first Friday he came home with the money.
The second Friday he came home with the money.
The third Friday was too much, and he didn't come
home until the money and the job were gone. After
such an occasion I was talking to him one day. He
said: "You know, I have never had anyone in my life
to help me." I felt it was such a cry for help. We of
the settled community, who are so quick to judge and
to condemn, should ask ourselves two questions. If
we had started as that young man did, with life
loaded against us from the start, would we have done
any better? Secondly, our attitude to this young man:
is it calculated to help him to rise above his difficulties, or to drive him deeper into them? I am glad to
say that he continues to make progress. He kept his
next job for more than a year, and a big change is
coming gradually in that family. Is it not families like
this that most need understanding help? Let us remember the words: "It is not the healthy who need
the doctor, but the sick. Go and learn the meaning
of these words: 'What I want is mercy, not sacrifice'"
(*Mt 9:12*).

Honesty

Some people think that all Travellers will steal.
Some, of course, do, just as some people in the settled
community do, but this does not mean that all are
dishonest. Many instances could be given, illustrating
their honesty. One young girl of fifteen had started in
her first job. On Friday she received her first pay
packet. It happened that the same day she found
someone else's pay packet lying on the floor. She took
it straight to the supervisor. Her mother was a widow,
and collected rags with a pram. They could very well
have done with the extra money, but this did not
affect her honesty.

For a while a Travelling family was camped near to us, and often came to see us. In the summer we had been weeding the onions, and one evening I went to look at them. About a quarter of the onions had been pulled up. They had not been taken, but were left lying on the ground. I was very annoyed. As I stood looking at them, I realised what had happened. In the weeding of the onions, they had got knocked about and many were lying sideways. It had ob-viously looked very tempting to these children to pull the onions the rest of the way out of the ground. I was afraid the remainder of the onions would share the same fate, so something had to be done.

I waited for a couple of days, and then met Paddy and his older sister coming over the field. "Paddy," I said, "there's something I want to show you." He was delighted, and we went off down the garden. When we got to the onions, he was very quiet. "Paddy," I asked, "who was with you when you pulled up the onions?" "I didn't pull them up," he said, "I was only watching." "Who was with you?" I said. "Bridget," he answered. "Paddy," I said, "you and I have always been great friends, but if you pull up my onions, we won't be friends any more. Your Daddy has potatoes and onions in his garden. I don't pull them up, and you're not to pull mine up." His older sister said: "I'll tell me Daddy and he'll bate him." "No," I said, "don't. This is between Paddy and me and he's not going to do it any more." Later I met Bridget and said the same thing to her. She is a won-derfully cheerful child. Nothing gets her down. She grinned happily all the time I was talking to her. However, she got the message and we had no more trouble with the onions.

Thinking over this incident, I realised that neither these children nor their parents had ever before had anywhere that they could plant anything and watch it grow. They had not really meant any harm, they had done a purely childish act. Had the family been antagonistic, they could have come back at night and taken the remainder of the onions, and there would have been nothing that I could have done about it, but as we were friendly they accepted what I said, and the rest of the onions grew to maturity.

In the autumn I was watching our few apples ripening, but one day noticed about half of them were gone. I suspected where they had gone, but as there were other possibilities I was not sure, so didn't want to say anything. One evening I was visiting Bridget and her family. She was chatting to me. They were about to move on to a new site, where they would have good accommodation and they would have a small garden. Bridget was telling me all the things she thought they would have in their garden. Finally, she said "Apples," and stopped and looked at me. I felt I was sure then where my apples had gone, and that she was unhappy about it, and wanted to tell me, if she could bring herself to. I said: "Yes, you could have apples in your garden." "I tasted one of your apples," she said. "I think you tasted more than one," I said, "didn't you?" "Yes," she said, and we had a little chat about taking things that belonged to other people. For a while I forgot about the apples, assuming that the lot had already been taken, but some weeks later I noticed there were still a number on the tree. Evidently, they had not been touched since our conversation.

When we remember how impressionable are the minds of children of this age, we realise how important it is how we treat these children now. How we treat them now, may well be how they treat us in later life. We can understand something of the meaning of the words of Jesus when he said: "Anyone who is an obstacle to . . . one of these little ones who have faith in me would be better drowned in the depths of the sea" (Mt 18:6).

Shortly after one of the first few families had moved into their caravan, the father was talking to me one day. He said: "We have never been as happy in our lives, as we are now. We had never had a chance in life, until you people gave us one." He was a builder's labourer, and added: "Of course, I don't tell the fellas where I'm working that I came off the road." "Why not?" I said. "There's nothing wrong with being on the road." "Ah but there is," he said, "there's people that think that if you're on the road, if you see something you want, you'll take it, whether it's yours or not." "Yes," I said, "I know there are people on the road like that; but they are not all on the road. We have people like that in the settled community too, and in any case, all the people on the road aren't like that." "Ah but," he said, "you know that. Other people don't, and they just think we're all the same. If the fellas found out, I would give up my job." "Don't do any such thing," I said, "if they find out, you stick to your guns and let them see that you're different." It was easy for me to say that. It would be another thing for him to do it. I could feel the struggle that was going on in his life, and the tremendous injustice that would be done to him, if he should fail, because of the stigma which we wrongly attach to all of these people.

Let us remember the words of our Lord when he was asked: "Which is the first of all the commandments?" We remember what he said. Then he added: "The second is this: You must love your neighbour as yourself" (Mk 12:31). Sometimes people say: "Well, if they would do this or that, we would feel differently about them." What we have to remember is this: our Lord did not wait for people to be perfect until he loved them. He loved them as they were, and in so doing, inspired and helped them towards a better life. Nearly 2,000 years ago, his Spirit touched men's hearts, and they became changed people. May the same Spirit touch our hearts today, giving us greater understanding of those born to a different way of life from our own, enabling us to see in all men, our brothers.

VICTOR E. H. BEWLEY *was born in 1912. On leaving school he joined Bewley's Cafés Ltd., where he is now Chairman and Managing Director. Married with three daughters and three grandchildren, he is a member of the Religious Society of Friends (Quakers) and Vice-Chairman of the National Council for Travelling People. In 1974 he was appointed by the Minister for Local Government as Adviser to the Minister on the Settlement of Travelling People.*

2 Life with the Travelling People

The camp-site

It is nearly four years now since I lived for six weeks
in an unofficial itinerant camp in County Galway.
The camp I stayed in was situated on a side road, off
the main Dublin-Galway road, approximately three
miles from Galway city. The passer-by might be
attracted by the picturesque view of a row of gaily
painted caravans, but on closer inspection would
probably be repelled by the dirt of the surroundings,
the crowd of ragged children and the stark poverty
in the faces of the older people. To the Travellers
camped there, the location of the camp had certain
advantages. With the exception of Big Tom, who had
not moved from the camp for two years, they had
been there for eight months and intended to move
for the summer—not a completely voluntary decision, as will be seen. It was close to a source of
water, not a very reliable one, but still useful, surrounded by fields, private property and Local
Authority property, a source of sticks for the fires and
grazing for the animals. The ground under the wattle
tents was dry due to prolonged use, except in heavy
rain. A wall afforded some shelter to the row of
caravans and tents without necessitating the three
distinct nuclear families living on top of each other.
It was close enough to the city and yet far enough out
to let them keep their animals.

The people and their possessions

In the camp I met Big Tom, his wife Maggie and

44

their children: Michael, aged 11 years, Mary, aged 9, Martin, aged 8, Maggie, aged 6, Davy, aged twenty months, and a baby aged six months who had been in hospital since birth and was not expected home. Their income was made up of Unemployment Assistance (£9. 18. 0 approx. per week) and Children's Allowance (£5. 6. 0 approx. per month).[1] Big Tom was also able to earn about £40 per annum from the sale of tin goods, and Maggie sold knitted goods which earned her about £30 per annum. They had very little income from begging. Their possessions consisted of one wagon, one shelter tent completely covered with waterproof, two horses, one chair, one old radio, some sheets of tin, a few tools, one frying-pan, one kettlebar, six tin cups and six tin plates, two cans for cooking, one knife, knitting needles, very little clothing and one cart.

Tom is a son of the Wards. He is a tinsmith and he occasionally obtains a sale for his goods. He made all the vessels[2] in the camp. Their shelter tent is his workshop and none of the children sleep in it. They all sleep on the floor of the wagon. Maggie rarely begs. This is attributed to laziness by the other women, but in fact Maggie seems to have unusual difficulty with the accommodative attitude of the begging woman. Consequently, her children and herself and Tom are very badly dressed. They are well fed, however, because he contributes most of his dole money to the groceries and is not a heavy drinker. Tom and Maggie are devoted to each other and their children; they are orientated to the settled world, perceptive about the changes that are overwhelming the Travellers, and are ambitious for their children. They have camped in the same place for two years so

[1]All social benefits mentioned have been increased since this study was done in 1970.

[2]Travellers' usual word for delph and pots and pans.

that their children can go to school and they watch
their progress with great interest, disappointed that
their daughter learns only catechism for which she is
kept in late every day, but pleased that their son
Michael "is a bit of a scholar".

Tom does a lot of work, making cups, milk cans
for sale to the farmers, painting his wagon and cart,
repairing things, and seeing to the horses. Maggie
cannot light a fire in their shelter tent because it is
not possible to tear a hole for smoke in waterproof.
Consequently, Maggie and her family can be seen
sitting in the ditch in every kind of weather, even
pouring rain, trying to light a fire and cook a meal.
Maggie seemed to resent the arrival of the others with
the winter and kept to herself most of the time,
although she was never openly unfriendly to the
others. Tom seemed to share her feelings but associ-
ated more with the others as they were his family, but
still not to the extent of going drinking with them.

One of the "others" was John Cash, a mentally
retarded Traveller, who was single. His possessions
consisted of a tent made of plastic bags and a tiny
piece of waterproof; a dog, Tony; a donkey, Film-
star; one suit of clothes and one set of sweep's brushes
which he did not know how to use. John received
Unemployment Assistance (£3. 13. 0. per week) and
paid Tom fifty shillings of this, for which Maggie
fed him and did her best to look after him. He collected old bottles and occasionally got some money
for them and from charitable sources. He was tolerated by the group, but teased unmercifully, especially
about marriage.

Meeting the families

The main group in the camp was made up of Big
Mammy and Daddy, Francis, Mary, Teresa, Ann and
her small sons Ned and Pat, Bridget (occasionally)

and her daughter Annie. Big Daddy received Unemployment Assistance (£6. 8. 0. per week approx.), and Big Mammy sold knitted goods which brought in about £50 a year. She also sold second-hand clothes and begged, though on a very limited scale. Ann received Children's Allowance (£1. 5. 6. per month). The sale of knitted goods brought her in about £50 a year, and she also obtained some cash from begging, and clothes which she re-sold. Mary and Teresa begged for money for family groceries, and also earned about £80 each per year from the sale of knitted goods. Bridget's only source of income was begging.

Big Daddy owned a wagon and two horses. He appeared to be in debt to the local money-lender for his wagon, and the horses were spoken of as the property of his youngest unmarried son Francis, but they were still Big Daddy's until Francis married. They had a shelter tent. The old couple slept in their wagon. Mary, Teresa and Annie slept on one side of the shelter tent amidst bags of wool and clothes, and Francis slept on the other side. The main group had nine tin cups, and eight tin plates, a frying pan, two cans for tea, four or five other canisters containing flour, sugar, a fishing rod and other such things. There was one large knife in this group and one spoon. They had one cart.

Ann's husband had left her two years previously, and she had a wagon of her own with a bed for herself and her sons. She also had two horses. An American woman who had met the Wards one summer supplied most of Ann's sons' clothes. Ann did not draw deserted mother's allowance either through ignorance of its existence, refusal or fear of refusal, or unwillingness to admit that she had been deserted.

Mary was 26 years of age and Teresa 18. Their only possessions were their clothes. They both knitted extensively and sewed nearly all their own skirts and aprons. Francis was 17 years of age. He was not eligible for any social benefits but worked in England every summer as a labourer and owned a fishing rod and a dog. Annie, a girl of 9 years, had been reared by Big Mammy since she was a baby. She was the daughter of Bridget who visited and left the camp regularly.

Then there were John, his wife Lizzie and their children: Winnie aged 12 years, John aged 11, Maggie aged 9, Bernie aged 8, Teresa aged 7, Martin aged 6, Ned aged 4, Lizzie aged 3 and Francis aged thirteen months. Their income was made up of Unemployment Assistance (£11. 0. 0. per week approx.) and Children's Allowance (£10. 11. 0. per month). Lizzie also begged when she was there. The family possessions consisted of one wagon, one shelter tent, one horse, one cart, one bicycle (property of the eldest son, Young John), a few tin utensils, one kettle, some clothes.

John was in debt to the money-lender for his wagon, but bought a second horse from the money-lender on a "hire purchase" arrangement. Lizzie was 12 years older than John and had three other children by a previous marriage. They did not live in the camp. She had left him on previous occasions in the past but she was not expected back this time. However, she did come back. John's children presented a sharp contrast to Tom's. They were badly fed and neglected and only one of them could go to school and she could only go sporadically because of the home circumstances.

Mrs Casey was a widow and received a widow's pension. She and her daughter Mary also managed to earn about £80 a year between them from the sale of knitted goods. The money for their groceries was obtained by begging. They had one wagon, some tin utensils, some clothes, and Mary dressed unusually well.

Bridget's income was derived entirely from begging in the street. When she left her husband, she had no other source of income at all, and possessed only the clothes she wore. She had six other children besides Annie: Tom aged 11, Cathleen aged 13, Bridget aged 8, Nan aged 6, John aged 5, and Kate aged 2. She is an alcoholic and spends most of her begging money on drink. Her husband is an emaciated wino who is badly in need of medical care, as are Bridget and the children. He mistreats her and the children, beating them, depriving them of food and shelter, and forcing the children to beg on the street for his wine and methylated spirits. Bridget often spends some time in the camp to avoid being beaten by him.

Breadwinners, foragers and workers

"Did you do good today, John?" asked Winnie, when she met him on his way out of town. "I did; I had luck," John replied, showing us a motley collection of dirty bottles. The notion of luck is very important in the Travellers' lives. The phrase "I hope you'll be lucky" follows you everywhere—into town, into marriage, into a venture of any kind. For many Travellers, luck in the form of a chance acquaintance often decides what they will eat.

Winnie and I were going to town to get Winnie's groceries. She had absolutely no money but she brought her shopping bag, which was the usual behaviour pattern among the girls. Her mother had been gone for four weeks, and Winnie had insisted defiantly that she hoped she would never return. Taking none of the children with her had hurt Winnie and caused tremendous ill-feeling towards Lizzie in the camp. Lately, she had been spending the begging money on food for herself and ignoring her hungry children. John was drinking heavily since her departure, heartbroken and ashamed; he was spending all his dole money on drink for himself and his friends. In his depressed and listless state, he hardly seemed to notice his hungry deprived children, who clamoured for his attention. At night, he would sit in his tent, drunk and crying, handing out sweets to his cowed children.

Fights had become very frequent as John reacted violently to every slight, real or imagined, against his wife. It was significant that the main group, his parents and sister, fed John every night on his return from the pub. This was his only meal of the day. However, they did not give even a slice of bread to Winnie and the children. At meal-time two or three of John's children would sit around the main fire, silently watching the food, and waiting hopefully to be given some. They were usually completely ignored. Occasionally, if Big Mammy was not present, they were given a slice of dry bread. As hard-hearted as this appears to be, the withholding of food was a pragmatic decision because they could not afford to feed nine extra mouths and they were not willing to relieve John or more specifically, Winnie, of her responsibility. If they were to feed them, it was very likely that more of their married children in similar difficulties would expect the same. In this desperate struggle for survival, no one could be allowed to give up. It was Winnie's job to "find" for the eight children, and we were on our way to town to "find".

"Finding" the groceries

Winnie went to various shops she knew and begged for food or money. I held the bags outside. After two hours of this, Winnie had collected six paper bags of bones and suet and a bag of over-ripe tomatoes, which she immediately started eating, and a bag of stale sausage meat. She got 2/6d. and bought cigarettes for Mary, as she had been told to. She also went to a shop owner who had told her he would give her a job. He told her she was too young for another two years and that she would have to learn to read and write before he could employ her. It was precisely the answer she had expected. Realising how hungry the children were, I bought the necessary groceries. Winnie promised to repay me, and did. "I'll ask my Daddy for a few pounds on dole day," she said.

The significant aspects of this incident were the acceptance without comment of the plight of John's children, even when they had barely eaten for three days, and the acceptance of the dole as the man's spending money, and the duty of the wife to "find" the groceries. Although the plight of the children was not discussed, the main family were keeping a close eye on events. They were obviously afraid that John would go and join his wife, leaving them with nine children to rear. His wife was attacked with great hostility inside the camp, but defended among outsiders (other Travellers). They regretted that the children had "gone very bad"; that is, they were unkempt, dirty and badly fed. Mary and Teresa helped Winnie with her many domestic chores.

The acceptance of the dole as the man's money to spend as he wished was not confined to John's family. The women spoke of the dole money as "money you could fall back on if you had to". Tom was the exception who contributed most of his money to the groceries. Travelling men have only been made eligible for the dole in very recent years. The travelling woman has traditionally "found for" the groceries, a reflection of the very insecure income of the man. It appears that many Travellers do not expect the dole money to continue, and so far many of them have incorporated it into their adaptive system of strict division of income.

The groceries of the Wards were very poor. Travellers generally seem to place a low value on food and do not think it worthy of comment if they have to eat little or nothing for a day or two. This is not to say that they do not feel hunger as the rest of the population does. The Wards ate twice a day; the food was generally of poor quality and quantity and very monotonous. It was impossible to imagine men surviving, let alone working as labourers on such a diet. In many, but not all cases, it was supplemented by drink—stout and wine—and by sweets in some cases.

"Tinker pubs"

Thursday was the best day of the week in the camp. It was dole day. Everyone was off to town early. The men and some of the women, the married women, collected the dole money and spent the day socialising at the three "tinker pubs". Mary and Teresa and possibly Ann went to town with their shopping bags. They begged on the street sometimes for a few hours, then went down to the pubs and occasionally got some of the men's dole money. Then the long-drawn-out process of getting the groceries started. The Travellers never shopped in the big supermarkets or "quality shops", as they call them. They could not read the labels on food in the supermarkets and they could not buy food in the small quantities they needed. They frequented the small dirty shops in the back streets where they knew the owners personally. Here they begged for left-over food and went from shop to shop looking for the best value in "a shilling's worth of meat".

All the travelling women in the city then left their parcels in a specific shop and went to talk to the crowds gathered at the pubs. Everyone in this group did not drink by any means. None of the unmarried people in this camp drank at all. On dole day, Big Tom usually hitched up his pony and cart and went to town with the children who were not at school. He collected his money, did the groceries, and joined the crowd at the pubs for a short while, had a few pints and then came home to Maggie. Someone went "shopping" almost every day except Sunday and Monday. Sometimes the process was much shorter if they had money left over from some source—begging money, payment for handcrafts, some dole money, etc.

It needs to be stated that the three "tinker pubs" were much more to the Travellers than places in which to get drunk, which is what settled people generally think of them. They are social centres in every sense. The proprietors of two of these pubs provided very necessary services for the Travellers. One of them was used as a standing address by every travelling family in the area, depending on which pub the family frequented and also which pub they would be served in. The owners of these pubs had a monopoly on the Travellers' trade and could lay down rules about which tribes they would serve. They kept messages for their customers, provided a letter-reading, and occasionally, a letter-writing service. Settled people who wanted to contact a Traveller could either find him at one of these pubs or leave a message with the owner, confident that it would be delivered. Travellers left messages for each other with the owners and found that they were always delivered. A Traveller could get a cup of tea in these pubs, the only places in the city where they could get one.

There are very few places in any town where Travellers can gather and socialise without running into trouble with the authorities. This they are allowed to do at the "tinker" pubs, situated in the back streets, avoided by the settled population. Here they gather and talk, keeping up with the news of interest to them, arranging matches, etc. Discrimination and prejudice not only mean that the pubs are almost the only entertainment allowed to Travellers; they also create the need in the Travellers to cling to each other in a way that settled people seem to find excessive. Settled people are very rarely seen in "tinker" pubs. Their owners depend entirely on the Travellers' trade. Despite the vast amount of drink that the Travellers are reported to consume, "tinker" pubs tend to look notoriously run-down.

Spending patterns

The material culture of the Travellers is extremely poor. Their property has to be confined to what they can take with them when travelling. This partly explains the importance of horses and donkeys to them. Besides being a quick way of calculating a man's wealth, they are an investment. Vans and cars are beginning to replace them now to a limited extent. Vans have the advantage of not needing grazing, but the substantial disadvantages of needing petrol, tax and insurance. They are a status symbol, a sign of wealth. The majority of Travellers would be ashamed now to arrive at a wedding, funeral or other gathering in a pony and cart, as the following incident illustrates:

Big Mammy and Daddy were invited to a niece's wedding, to take place in a town some twenty miles away. Next day they were visited by a group of Travellers with a van. When asked if they were going to the wedding, they replied that they had no way of going, despite the fact that they had a horse and cart. After a good deal of discussion about the price of petrol, the owner of the van offered to drive them. He drove the whole family in two trips the day of the wedding, and, of course, was paid.

Big Tom was the only one who would drive his pony and cart to town. The others would walk or get the bus occasionally. There is a practical reason for this, too, namely that it is becoming very dangerous for a man with a pony and cart on the roads, with the volume of modern traffic. There have been many road accidents involving Travellers in carts, and consequently they are afraid.

Very little of their income is spent on capital goods. Many Travellers are in debt to money-lenders for their wagons, horses, etc. At matches, dowries are often settled by arrangements with these money-lenders, although the dowries are very little. The vast majority of the Travellers seem to be outside the consumer society. Their material needs at present, in this particular camp anyway, have been confined to an alarmingly primitive level. Their evaluation of the necessities of life is extremely low. The older Travellers particularly are unaware of the existence of a variety of consumer goods. Many such goods have no relevance to their lives at present.

Growing-up patterns

The poor material culture is reflected in the children's vocabulary, and indeed in the vocabulary of all Travellers. The children's lack of familiarity with things settled people take for granted, e.g. furniture, tooth-paste, forks, a variety of foods and toys, etc., tends to retard them at school where all the words and the lessons come from a settled cultural background. Their pronunciation also tends to be poor, partly as a result of their social isolation and partly because all Travellers learn gammon or Shelta as well as English as babies. These factors may lead a teacher to consider travelling children unintelligent, and she may consequently ignore them, increasing the already acute sense of inferiority that Travellers feel with regard to "the quality" (the settled population). There seems to be a strong case for special remedial schools for travelling children aimed at bridging the gap between the settled culture and that of the Travellers.

The young people in the camp went to the pictures fairly often. This is a growing entertainment alternative to the traditional drinking. They were all orientated to modern trends, like pop-music, and took a personal interest in the pop stars, loved Westerns because of the many links with their cultural background—the wagons, the horses, the camp-fires, etc. They preferred action to dialogue in the pictures, and good guys versus bad guys to love stories.

Yet they remained spectators to modern trends in real life, particularly the girls. Very little money was spent on clothes. The girls occasionally got suitable skirts when begging, but the clothes they got were usually considered too modern (i.e. immoral) for travelling girls to wear. Consequently, they spent some money buying material for skirts, aprons, lining for the insides of the wagons and for the tents. This money was each girl's own money. Everyone has his own money. There is no sharing of money at all and even between husband and wife, sharing money is minimal.

Mary and Teresa both have to buy a considerable amount of the family groceries. In fact, nearly all their income seems to go on groceries. Big Mammy occasionally buys the groceries, and Ann too. Francis is completely exempted from contributing to the household expenses and a lot of campwork too. Big Daddy contributes nothing to the groceries. Occasionally, the girls buy something for themselves, e.g. Teresa saved for a long time from her knitting money and bought herself a leatherette coat, well below her knees in length, of course, but still considered short enough to cause considerable controversy.

The items of capital expenditure which are valued

and bought when possible are as follows in the order of importance the Travellers assign to them: vans or cars, lorries, television (if possible, for example on serviced sites), radios, trailers, horses and donkeys. Clothes would come very near the bottom of the list, except in the cases of the young single people.

From dole day until the following Monday or Tuesday, the "lads"—Big Mammy and Daddy, Ann, John, and Lizzie upon her return—went drinking every day, sometimes spending all day in town, sometimes only a few hours, and returned drunk or semi-drunk every night. All the "lads" were married, one deserted, one semi-deserted. Marriage is the turning point in the Travellers' lives. It is probably the most important status symbol in their lives, which are so closely bound to the themes of birth, marriage and death. Marriage also represents a definite commitment to the travelling life, to the almost inevitable pattern of a large number of children, sickness and early death.

The unemployment of the man, resulting sometimes in a loss of initiative and a loss of a sense of responsibility, the dependence on his wife's begging, prevalent in the poorer group, results in a fatalism, a present-time orientation that at least allows him to enjoy the pleasure of the moment. The married Traveller turns inward to the travelling community from frustration, and clings closely to the traditional beliefs and values of the Travelling People in search of security and meaning for his life.

The "quality"

Defensive beliefs about settled people grow, i.e. settled people are cold and hard-hearted, murder their wives and enemies with impunity, have an inordinate amount of wealth, and barely concealed homicidal tendencies towards Travellers. This last belief was brought home very forcibly when, in a discussion between myself, a friend of mine, and Young John aged 11, Young John proceeded to tell a story with great seriousness and sincerity about a "quality lady" who had given himself and his cousin a lift in the back of her car and then attempted to murder them by gassing them. The discussion was about hitch-hiking, the fear or fantasy expressed was completely unexpected and unsuspected, and Young John quite obviously thought that the event as he interpreted it was a real possibility. When asked why the lady would want to kill them, he replied: "Because we was Travellers."

These Travellers, born in the sub-culture of poverty, by a mixture of luck and outside help at the crucial time seem to retain a sense of personal dignity and worth and do not need the constant reassurance of their peers to face life. Objectively, the difference in the standard of living between Tom's family and John's existed, but it was certainly not enough to in-duce John—who was heartbroken and ashamed by his wife's behaviour and was often unable to face his deprived children, especially the contempt of his eldest daughter, which mirrored that of his wife—to leave the security and the sense of adequacy bestowed by his drinking. The sacrifices made by Tom were too much for John, a man with a deep sense of inferiority, so much that he was unable to look straight at a quality person because he felt they would see all his deficiencies, of which he was too painfully aware. His sense of alienation and unworthiness made him won-der, even when drunk, about my willingness to associate with his daughter, whereas Big Tom would accept my friendship with the quiet dignity of an equal relationship.

Only when he was really drunk could John achieve enough self-confidence to sing (he has a very good voice), or even express an opinion in my presence. The young people disapproved of their parents' spending habits and resented visitors who tended to increase the heavy drinking. The parents in turn disapproved of their children's spending habits, afraid of too close a relationship with settled people— at the pictures for example, especially the girls.

Work

None of the men in the group were employed while I was there although they had all worked at some stage of their lives. Both Big Tom and John had limps as the result of accidents on labouring sites. Big Daddy had worked as a tinsmith, a sweep, in bars and at various other jobs. Work presents a big threat to the illiterate travelling man. It is easier to get a job in England but there are more strange things to cope with. Travellers, because of their isolation, are prone to prejudice. Fear of "the black people" is a common enough reason for return from England.

The travelling man who gets an ordinary employee job is afraid that his deficiencies will be too great and that he will not be able for it. From experience, they have learned the folly of taking hard long-hour jobs for small pay and all agree that it is "foolish to work too hard". They have difficulty coping with an impersonal employee-employer relationship and have great difficulty adjusting to the discipline of the clock. Pre-industrial work attitudes still exist in the indigenous setting among the older men. In the indigenous setting, their felt needs are few, although their objective needs are many. Higher aspirations pre-date understanding the logic of a well-developed work ideology in which people bow to the necessity of regular work for the duration of the best part of their lives. The travelling man's expectation of failure and his fear of it is very acute.

The kind of work he can get confirms his sense of inferiority.

Travellers therefore prefer if possible to avoid the unequal competition of the labour market by working in family teams of Travellers, collecting scrap, horse-dealing, or laying tarmacadam. These businesses require an initial outlay of capital which the poorer Traveller has not got. For the poorer Traveller, work is just one part of the whole economic enterprise. He takes work and leaves it, having no commitment to it at all, as luck dictates. Paradoxically, bad luck may cause him to leave his job unexpectedly. A Traveller lost £200 at work in a factory. He immediately left his job, leaving his employer baffled. He expected him to work harder to regain the money he had lost. To the Traveller, the loss was the sign of defeat he had been waiting for. He expects to be dismissed, to be unable for the work, to make mistakes, and sometimes he goes to great lengths to prove himself right.

The tarmacadam crews appear to do good business. They work on a family basis and hire relatives and friends for extra help. Scrap-dealers trade with bigger scrap dealers, and so on. There are no organised criminal concerns offering careers in crime. "Tinkers" who commit anything more than petty offences seem to be invariably caught and given lengthy sentences. However, there are certain tribes who make their living by exploiting other poorer and more defenceless Travellers. Most of these are illegal money-lenders who provide a necessary service for the travelling community by supplying wagons, horses, etc. on the hire-purchase arrangements. They are as illiterate as their clients and consequently no accounts are kept on either side, making it very difficult for the Traveller to get out of a money-lender's grip. Payment is enforced by violence and threats of violence. Some of the apparently motiveless fights or "drunken brawls" among Travellers are, in fact, the money-lenders at work.

A very few tribes extract money by violent means from other Travellers with no pretext of a business arrangement at all. These tribes and the money-lenders are well known and feared within the travelling community. They are part of the economic adaptation to inherited poverty.

The economics of poverty can be mercilessly exploitive. The stronger and wealthier benefit from the continued exploitation of the poorer and weaker Travellers. It is almost impossible for settled people or authorities to get any information about these activities. The extreme alienation of the Travellers from the wider society can be clearly seen in their preference to be exploited by someone they know and can understand rather than to have recourse to a legal system they have reason to fear and do not understand.

Jobs for the girls

Travelling girls are beginning to work to an appreciable extent. They find it easier to get work than their men in many areas. The reasons for this are the present employment situation and the greater willingness of people to employ tinker girls than tinker men. They seem to feel the women are more capable of rehabilitation and are less frightening and tend to be more accommodative than the men. They work as waitresses, maids in hospitals and private houses, and in similar occupations.

Three travelling girls worked as maids in the local hospital. One was married and had left her husband and child. They dressed in modern clothes and visited the camp often. The older people disapproved of them, especially their giggly ways and "settled-girl" habits and of their interest in Francis. Mary had often expressed a strong desire to get a job in a hospital and was very interested in their account of their pay and conditions, which were unusually good, as they reported them. Mary wondered should she try for a job. Her fear of refusal and Big Mammy's disapproval, expressed in disbelief about the quoted pay and conditions, finally prevented her. Various justifications for not taking the job were made—fear of blood, operating theatres, loneliness of having to sleep in, difficulty of working for nuns, getting up so early. Big Mammy was afraid that Mary would completely forget her station in life if she got the job and would join the settled society, taking a source of income from the family and rejecting them. Mary was afraid she would be refused, especially with the three girls as unsympathetic witnesses, and that the work would be very hard and tedious. She had worked as a waitress, very long hours for very little pay and she did not want to repeat the experience.

Teresa too expressed interest in the jobs, but her sense of inferiority even regarding the three girls, who now considered themselves to be very superior, prevented her from applying. They had learned to expect rejection and failure from the settled world and especially from the settled world of work.

Relationships

On a warm day, Big Tom and Maggie would sit sleeping in the ditch on the side of the road, Maggie's head on Tom's shoulder, his arm around her and a child's colouring book in his other hand. Evidence of his painstaking efforts to follow the numbers and learn something could be seen on the pages. This couple were devoted to each other, almost inseparable, sharing a deep personal friendship and love (although they would never use such an extravagant word), grown out of their isolation and sharing of hardships.

They are the ideal travelling couple. They represent what every young couple set out to be, but many never achieve. Young travelling couples often travel alone for some time and, according to their personalities, may continue to travel alone for years. They are then thrown back on each other's company, isolated socially from the settled world, and the result is often deeply attached middle-aged couples (old age for them).

Matches are made with the help of professional matchmakers. It is very possible that travelling children are sometimes matched off to their cousins from birth. Marriages between first, second, and third cousins are the rule rather than the exception. Matches are less formal than they used to be in settled society. After a wedding, a match is made for the next single girl in her tribe. The girl has the right to refuse the match. Mary turned down five matches before I went to stay in the camp and turned down a sixth while I was there. The boy, too, had the right of refusal in a case where the match was not initiated by him. Dowries were settled in a flexible way. Someone must provide a "spree" for the wedding, enough money for drink for the company. This is usually the man but this matter is flexible. The girl's parents often provide a donkey or a pony and harness and the boy provides the cart. This is all that is considered necessary. Gifts from settled people are fairly common at tinker weddings in rural areas, e.g. clothes, food, utensils, money. The bride's clothes are occasionally provided by a settled person who knows her, which accounts for the sometimes bizarre dress of the poor bride.

A travelling girl is expected to be ashamed on her wedding day. The party stay with the young couple all night to make sure the bride does not try to go home and because the young couple bring them luck. Then the young couple set out to travel by themselves for a while. Church weddings are the rule now but the church ceremony is not regarded as the biggest part of the event and many of the older people are not officially married. The marriage relationship is remarkably close in theory to that in other low income groups. However, consideration of the married states in this particular camp—one desertion and two semi-desertions (one of these has not been discussed yet)—illustrates that the relationship was often very turbulent in practice. The lives of husbands and wives are not too sharply segregated; except in the sphere of work, and where the men are unemployed this is not a major sphere.

However, an exclusively male group exists. When visitors came to the camp, after a few minutes' general conversation, the men would move away from the women and often spend hours sitting and talking. They gossip continuously, even more than the women. Their conversation appears to centre around much the same topics as low-income men everywhere— drink, gambling, eluding the Gardaí, fights, encounters with the money-lenders, horses, vans, cars, women, money made on a trick or a gamble, encounters with the settled world and the usuals of births, marriages and deaths. Occasionally they go to town in a group but there is little or no segregation of the sexes in the pubs, for example. There is a women's group out of necessity, but this is completely disorganised and centres around the men's group. On sites where the men's group flourishes, the men may be absent most of the day—at the ball alley, playing cards or just sitting around. The women then complain strongly of being virtually deserted.

The closeness of the marriage relationship is well illustrated in the reaction to separation. John became extremely depressed, listless and apathetic when Lizzie left him. Ann seemed depressed very often and Bridget was an alcoholic and chronically depressed.

Joseph Murphy, a friend of the group, had a bad criminal record—petty theft mostly, graduating to breaking and entering. He spent a great deal of time in jail. While he was in jail, his wife became extremely depressed, stopped taking care of herself and drank heavily. On his release, she changed completely, although by middle-class standards he did not treat her well. When he re-entered prison, she again lapsed into deep depression. Marriage as a relationship is very highly regarded. It is a status symbol—the most important one in travelling society.

There were two single men in the group, both psychologically abnormal—one a Traveller and one a tramp, Old Tom, who lived in a shack up the road. Tramps tend to mix socially with Travellers but try to keep a certain distance between themselves and the Travellers. This does not exempt them from the low opinion of the Travellers because they are not married and have no women or children. Both of these men were teased continually, almost invariably about women. Their abnormality, or "softness", was defined by their inability to get a wife, a fact which consequently haunted the two unfortunate men to a remarkable degree.

Match-making

During my stay, a match was made between myself and John Cash. It proved very instructive to me but upsetting to poor John who took it seriously. Matches between cousins have the advantages that the couple know each other well, having usually camped alongside each other at some stage in their lives, and that the match is kept within the tribe, reducing the chances of inter-tribe conflict which is always present. Matches are rarely made between complete strangers —that is, a couple who have not known each other at some stage. The difference in the ages of the partners

may be great. The last prospective husband offered
to Mary was 19 and she is 26. John's wife, formerly a
widow, is 12 years older than him. Widows and
widowers generally remarry unless they were very old
at the time of their partner's death. Thirty-five is old
for travelling women and around fifty for men.

Marriage or consensual unions between deserted
wives and single men, or couples from otherwise
broken marriages, or mutual swopping of partners
do occur. There was one such union in this area and
they may be more common than generally supposed.
There appears to be a bigger proportion of travelling
men than travelling women at present. Marriage con-
fers status on both partners and gives them a recognised place in the community. Ambiguity about roles
develops in the case of single people who remain
single after the sanctioned marriage age.

Mary was an example of this role-uncertainty. Her
health was not good and she had been warned of the
danger to her health of having too many children.
She is unusually perceptive of the outside world, possibly as a result of her lengthy confinements in hospital, and she is orientated to the settled society. She
did not want to marry a man who was likely to be
immature and punishing. She shared her brother's
(Big Tom's) sense of personal worth and dignity, and
possessed the subtle sense of humour of the travelling
people to a very high degree. She had not found a
match that suited her yet. The health hazard involved
in marriage would have been dismissed by her parents
with the fatalistic reasoning that she would die if it
was God's will and that there was nothing she could
do about that. Within the extended family, Mary did
a disproportionate amount of the work, paid for a
disproportionate amount of the groceries and her
authority was constantly undermined by her married
sisters. She did not drink and a fight ensued the one

time she decided to accompany Teresa, Francis and myself to the pictures. She came however.

Once married, both men and women are subject to close scrutiny in their relationships with other men and women. Both sexes tend to be extremely jealous. The man retains much of his freedom which is somewhat restricted in man-woman relationships all his life. Courtship does not exist, at least in the usual sense. Sexual play is common enough in the parents' absence when the opportunity arises or in their presence at parties for weddings, matches and wakes sometimes. Sexual awareness comes early and sexual play and talk is common among the children. A close eye is usually kept on single girls but the boys' freedom is unrestricted except with regard to other Travellers' daughters, of course. Travelling men, because they do not dress differently from settled men, can sometimes pass as rural settled men and attend dances, etc. even when married, at times, and date settled girls. Francis explained to me that he only went out with them once because they would find out he was a Traveller if the relationship was continued. Marriages between settled girls and travelling men do occur but not the reverse.

All these marriages are not the result of matchmaking. When a boy and girl are noticed taking an interest in each other, a wedding is quickly arranged if the parents approve of the match. If they do not, they may try to prevent the relationship from continuing. The young people may then run away together to force the match and attempts to bring them back will be made. If they go a second time, they are usually allowed to marry. Romantic love is beginning to make a self-conscious appearance, especially in Dublin, but many young Travellers are confused about the dating pattern of settled people. As I tried to understand their marriage pattern, they were trying to understand mine and finally Francis asked me why it was "I often hear of quality people walking out for years without getting married". The explanation about economic circumstances made no sense at all to him. These Travellers all thought that settled people were extremely promiscuous.

The apparently rigid sexual code is the strictly enforced double standard of rural patriarchal society. Single girls are chaperoned by brothers in places where they are likely to meet other travelling or non-travelling men. At the pictures, where we could only go if Francis was going, if there were travelling men present, the girls would have to leave before the end of the film, on Francis's insistence, to avoid meeting them. Men and women, single and married, mix freely at the camps and especially at parties, but not away from the family in the indigenous rural setting. In the formal structure of man-woman relationships, the society is highly patriarchal just as it is in rural Ireland. In day-to-day affairs, it is matriarchal.

The men tend to be preoccupied with their masculinity. They are at least as fussy about their appearance as their women and often much more so. Within the male group, masculinity is gauged in terms of physical prowess, ability to fight, lack of fear, and more recently, driving ability. Boys on the fringes of the men's group, like Young John, are criticised for being "just an old girl" if they do not want to fight or if they act in some way that is considered feminine.

The women have a martyr-complex, which is not without objective foundations in the Travellers' world. In a sense, the men are one step removed from the struggle to wrest an existence from the settled world each day. The women act as buffers between them and the settled world, which accounts for the sometimes totally unrealistic statements made by travelling men to welfare agencies, etc. The woman's accommodative attitudes tend to be more highly developed than those of the men, who seek a more equal relationship with settled people. Travelling girls are reared to serve the men and the men tend to be demanding and aggressive with the women, while being dependent on them in many ways. The men are believed to be superior just by being males and the women are expected to be submissive.

Wife-beating is fairly common but husband-beating is not unknown either. The wife sometimes seems to interpret her husband's beating as a sign of affection—only, however, if she has been behaving "badly" especially to attract his attention, but not in the case of being beaten regularly by him when he is drunk. The responsibility for the children rests in practice with the women in the camp, although the men have a part to play in theory. The traditional protest of a travelling woman, short of leaving her husband, is to burn his property, the wagon. The married travelling woman who leaves her husband or is left by him is in a socially dangerous position if she is not accepted by an extended family group or does not find an alternative, which she usually does. If she does not, she is likely to be seen as an available sexual object by travelling men and sometimes does resort to prostitution in the wider society. The men regard the women as their property and generally speaking the women and children suffer most in the deprivations of their lives.

Parent-child relationship, pattern of child-rearing

Travelling society is adult-centred. It has been said that travelling children lead an idyllic life, with plenty to do, performing meaningful tasks in their lives, secure with the constant presence of their parents, unburdened by worries about school or the need to compete and succeed. There is some truth in this description but it is not the total picture. Children are an unqualified blessing, their birth is not planned, no plans are made for their lives, their arrival is accepted fatalistically, part of the natural cycle of events to which their lives are so closely bound. Travelling children as children are neither seen nor heard by their parents for a substantial part of their lives. They are miniature adults, allowed to stay up at adult parties and events of all kinds, to drink with their parents from a very early age and talk to them on an equal footing. The child-like activities of their lives take place outside the parents' interest or supervision.

During my stay, there were twenty-three children in the camp; six of these, Bridget's children, arrived at the beginning of my third week there, went home and returned again. This was a large number of children to have on a road. The problems created by this number of children would have been worse were it not for the two single girls in the extended family group. When Bridget arrived with the six children, Teresa regretted the fact that their road was turning into a road "full of widow-women and children". In fact, there was only one widow on the road and her daughter was not a child. She was referring to the number of broken families.

"Little young children"

Travelling children are treated to a mixture of indulgence and complete lack of interest in most of their activities. Babies are loved and indulged fiercely, although Travellers rarely use the word baby, perhaps because it denotes a degree of helplessness they cannot allow to anyone. "Little young child" is the preferred expression. "Little young children" are fussed over by everyone and usually become the full-time domestic responsibility of an older sister if there is one old enough—that is, 6 years old or older. John's baby Francis, aged thirteen months, was the responsibility of Teresa, aged 7. Maggie, aged 9, and Winnie, aged 12, helped her but were themselves burdened with other tasks. When Lizzie returned, Teresa continued to mind the baby and Lizzie helped her at times. "Little young children" are often not allowed to crawl at all, a very pragmatic decision for children living on the roads. Toilet training is dealt with simply and efficiently. Babies of both sexes wear little dresses without pants and spend most of the time outside the tents with their "little mothers", until they are toilet trained which is accomplished by a simple process of collective teaching by the other children.

Occasionally, settled women passing the camp were horrified at the semi-nakedness of the young children, interpreting it as blatant cruelty to children. They sometimes stopped to complain, but failed to appreciate that putting nappies, etc. on little children even if they had them (which they had not) would have created problems that settled people could not even begin to imagine. The fact that the young child was not allowed to crawl greatly increased the burden on his little mother. She had to carry him everywhere and hold him continuously during his waking hours. As soon as he could walk (and his little mother had a strong incentive to teach him), he was absorbed into the children's group where he was collectively watched.

The group of children impinged on the adult world only to be washed (five or six times a day), fed, given tasks and put to bed. They were present as an integrated part of the gathering at the two meals of the day, morning and late evening. Their contributions to the conversation, if they made any, were treated the same way as an adult contribution—even from little children of two years old and up. If they got restless or started fighting, they were promptly told to "go and play on the turf" even if it was raining heavily outside or was past eleven at night.

On the other hand, children were never excluded from adult events such as parties and never went to bed before their parents. Little boys of two years and up were given a bottle of stout at family parties and all the children witnessed fights and other adults' events. Their natural mother and father too were often out in town all day, except Big Tom and Maggie. One of the two girls, Mary or Teresa, usually stayed in the camp, cleaning the camp and supervising the children. They usually ignored the children completely unless they wanted some task performed or some event of a serious nature took place among the children. The children were allowed tremendous freedom to play with a few restrictions: they were forbidden to go near the main road, tell tales on each other, etc. Only once during my stay was one of the young children taken begging, when Ann borrowed John's youngest daughter to go begging for clothes. The older girls sometimes begged for money for sweets and in the case of John's children for food.

Big Tom's children had a very close relationship with their parents—again, the ideal relationship between parents and children in the travelling community. Once, on dole day, I accompanied Big Tom, Maggie and the children to town on the pony and cart. Tom tied the horse to a "no-parking" sign and remarked that those posts were very handy for the horses. (The complete illiteracy of the Travellers is sometimes difficult to appreciate in all its ramifications.) We went to the tinker pub, talked for a while to the gathering, and then Tom bought a crate of stout and took it outside to start the day. All the children, even the youngest—aged twenty months—had their own bottle. As the day wore on, Maggie left to do the groceries, taking some of the children with her, and returned some time later. By evening, parents and children were singing. We returned to the camp late in the evening.

Discipline

Parental discipline tends to be extremely sporadic. The same misdeed often invokes different responses at different times, depending entirely on the parents' mood. While the natural parents are present, members of the extended family do not punish the children and even in the absence of the parents, rarely do. The child's misdeeds often pass without comment from parents preoccupied with other worries. Threats are made very often but rarely carried out, and when they are it is often the result of the parent being in a bad mood rather than any particular misdeed on the child's part.

Physical punishment is used. Travelling children adapt to this situation by only obeying orders that seem likely to be physically enforced. This reluctance to obey commands continues right through the life cycle, and is extremely striking. A request is made or a command given. No one moves or even appears to have heard it. If it is repeated with sufficient force, action usually results. Often the request is simply dropped and repeated some time later. This situation is the cause of many rows, Travellers generally being reluctant to obey commands or perform tasks if they are not in the mood, unless they are forced to. This appears to be the result of the child-rearing pattern, where discipline does not follow any recognisable logic and children do not expect to be punished on any abstract principles of justice or strictly according to a set of understandable rules. Rules do exist but often a particular rule is an adaptation to a particular situation. In fact, Travellers often seem remarkably reluctant to interfere with their children's behaviour even when the Gardaí remind them to do so.

The segregation of the children's lives allows them to insulate activities that might merit punishment from their parents. Parents do not play with their

children; rather the children are allowed to partici-
pate in the parents' world on an equal footing.
Demanding and aggressive behaviour is welcomed
from the boys as a sign of masculinity. The same
behaviour is not tolerated from the girls who are
initiated at an early age into camp duties. They are
reared to serve the men, but the single girls do this
reluctantly. The boys have tasks too. They collect
sticks for the fire every day and attend to the horses.
They model themselves very consciously on their
fathers, uncles and grandfathers, adopting the pre-
occupation with their masculinity from a very early
age. The mothers tolerate a surprising amount of self-
assertive behaviour from their young sons and often
go to great lengths to prevent frustrating them,
especially around the crucial self-assertive years of two
and three. Temper tantrums are very common at this
age among travelling children and the parent often
goes to extraordinary lengths to prevent them, while
at other times, ignoring them completely. Attempts to
prevent temper tantrums apply to boys and girls.

Control over the girls is very much increased as
they get older. A girl's freedom to play as she wishes
is restricted as her camp duties are increased. If she
is one of the eldest of a large family, her life will not
change very much as she approaches adolescence, as
her childhood will have been taken up with domestic
duties anyway. If she is the youngest of a large family,
however, the change can be traumatic. Teresa, the
youngest child of thirteen in the main Ward family,
spoke to me about her childhood and how happy she
had been and how she had been a tomboy, doing
everything her brother did. She had found it hard to
adjust to the passive, submissive role of a travelling
woman and, in fact, was much more lively than her
sister Mary or even Winnie.

The mother is in charge of the day-to-day discipline of the children and the father is called in as a

last resort. The father's authority over the children is absolute when he is present to exercise it or when he chooses to, which is not very often as the children are regarded as the woman's responsibility. After about the age of eleven years, the mother loses authority over her sons who openly defy her wishes. Father and son then have a very close relationship, the father treating his son as a friend, teaching him his knowledge of the world, and formerly, passing on his craft to him. The crafts are not passed on any longer. Sons tend to have great respect for their fathers and all the men tend to leave the day-to-day affairs and decisions to the women. If the father is absent, or absent most of the time, or unable for some reason to carry on this relationship with his son, as John was for some time, it will be done by a male relative in the extended family; e.g. Francis took Young John with him everywhere, taught him to handle horses, to fish, what tasks to perform for the women, etc. Big Daddy acted as a father to Ann's children, but a problem will arise when they reach this important stage in their lives as he will most likely be dead.

Adolescence

There does not appear to be an adolescent "culture" among the Travellers in the indigenous setting. The adolescent crisis of the boys is handled as described. Problems arise when the adolescent children are kept at school and there is ambiguity about their future roles. Big Tom kept his 11-year-old son and 10-year-old daughter at school, leaving Maggie and himself with more tasks to perform than Travellers with children of these ages normally have. However, no problems had arisen yet. Michael's (Tom's son) literacy annoyed the older Travellers at times as he had not the tact to avoid making them feel inferior with his display of knowledge. Nevertheless, it was very highly prized.

The desire for literacy in the camp was overwhelming. My caravan was besieged every day with children who wanted to learn to write. I spent hours teaching Mary, Teresa, Francis and Winnie to write their names, at their request. They brought old newspapers and magazines for me to read to them. At night the men would sometimes get boys' comics and sit around the fire, trying to make out the story from the pictures. School-going children were questioned anxiously every day on their return from school about what they had learnt.

The frustration of this learning desire in some schools is particularly depressing when one considers that many travelling children have only a few short months in school before family circumstances force them to leave forever. All the young people felt their deficiency very keenly in this regard although Travellers generally object to boys staying at school "after their confirmation" because by then they are young men and going to school is not a masculine activity.

Adolescent Travellers slip easily into the clearly defined roles set out for them. There does not seem to be an identity crisis in the indigenous setting. The totally separate lives of young and old, common in settled urban societies at present, hardly exists. The young people go to the pictures more often but the whole family tends to be interested, in a very personal way, in the pop stars the young people recognise on the radio, and there is no generation gap with separate styles in clothes, etc.

Fathers and sons tend to be very friendly, the father giving his son the benefit of his experience, the son respecting him. The relationship between mothers and daughters is a less happy one. Control over the daughters is much more strict than over the sons; it is exercised by the mother in the normal course of events and the daughter has more work to do than the son and more to contribute financially to the family. Travelling children become aware of the hard facts of their lives at a very early age and tend to be much more worldly-wise than settled children, as their parents can only provide minimal protection from the harsh circumstances of their lives.

They do not play games with set rules or use concepts like "fair play". They play "tent" instead of "house" and in fact by far the majority of these games, like behaviour, is role-playing, modelled on their parents and the people around them in the camp. They have few toys, if any, and play with old prams used to collect water and with the babies. Very often it is noticeable that a brother and sister of close ages—the boy a little older—are inseparable. He takes his sister everywhere with him and plays with her continuously. This is a very interesting relationship and it is formally recognised in the match-making process. Sister and sister-in-law are expected to be jealous of each other and traditionally, a ritual relationship is established between them.

The extended family

The practical extended family does not necessarily include all the eligible members. Members of an extended family who interact frequently with each other are recruited to the group on the basis of compatibility and practical considerations, such as ability to move beside the group, etc. In a marriage involving two separate tribes, the couple will interact more with one of the extended families, the choice depending on the same factors as mentioned above. Sometimes a couple avoid both families. After travelling alone for some time, the couple usually return to the extended family for a while, but this matter is very flexible. Family ties are very close, partly as a result of their social isolation and partly because of historical reasons.

There were only two "outsiders" in the extended family group of the Wards in the camp studied, leaving aside John Cash and Mrs Casey and her daughter. They were Maggie, Tom's wife, and Lizzie, John's wife. On Lizzie's return, she avoided interaction with the extended family and interacted frequently with Maggie. These two women were in a disadvantageous position socially, both coming from separate tribes to the Wards, both without kinsmen in the group to support them. Maggie avoided too close interaction with the extended family all the time, as Lizzie did at first on her return, but quickly returned to drinking with them. Both women were constantly criticised in their absence, Lizzie particularly, of course.

Tasks were divided in a highly standardised way between the various members of the group. Each nuclear family was a social unit, performing its own tasks with some overlapping. The domestic duties in the camp were performed most of the time by the older single girls. The married women and the men, except Tom and Maggie, went to town on average four days a week, all day, and returned about 11.30 p.m. Mary, Teresa, Winnie and her younger sister Maggie did the work such as sweeping the road, fetching water, cooking and preparing meals, cleaning out the wagons and tents, cleaning the vessels, minding the children, and getting the groceries. Two girls usually went to town most days for the groceries, leaving one to mind the children and do the domestic chores. The married women sometimes did the groceries and always took over from the single girls in preparing and cooking the meals when they were there. The married women delegated the tasks to the single girls who in turn delegated as many as possible to the children, especially the girls. The married women did some begging in town, traded in second-

LIFE WITH THE TRAVELLING PEOPLE

hand clothes, begged from door to door for clothes and spent a good deal of time at the gatherings around the pubs. The presence of two single girls of Mary's and Teresa's ages was unusual and no doubt affected the allocation of domestic duties.

Big Mammy had a controlling function, in charge of all under her roof. She made most of the decisions affecting their day-to-day lives, even in such matters as tethering the horses, which are the man's responsibility. When she was present, she dealt with the Gardaí, the Inspector from the I.S.P.C.C. and all other outside agencies, interpreting their function for the group within a traditional framework. She did not interfere in the affairs of the two distinct nuclear families living separately in the group. However, she criticised Lizzie in John's presence and produced a row about this affair very often. She treated Big Daddy with contempt especially in his absence. She was much younger than he and had had thirteen children, of whom eight were living. At least one of her daughters-in-law was as old as herself, approximately 58 years old. Big Mammy decided who the extended family could help and how.

Bridget, a married daughter with seven children, lived on the other side of town. As previously mentioned, she was married to an emaciated alcoholic and was an alcoholic herself. He was permanently intoxicated and beat Bridget and the children, and forced his children to beg on the streets every day for money for his drink. Bridget often spent some time in the camp to avoid being beaten by him.

On the Wednesday of the second week I was there, Big Mammy and Ann were discussing Bridget and blaming everything on her husband, of course. They were particularly angry that the children had to beg on the street. Travellers are extremely fond of their children, although circumstances sometimes force them to treat them in a way that seems

cruel to affluent, settled people. Bridget arrived
at the camp that night with her eldest daughter,
Cathleen, following an exceptionally bad fight with
her husband. He had locked the children out again
and was in the wagon in a drunken stupor with some
of his drinking friends. Francis was sent out to protect
the children.

Next day Mary, Cathleen and I went to town and
collected the remaining five children from the pub
where their mother was drinking. Then we all set out
for the Ward's camp. Bridget's eldest son, Tom, aged
11, hesitated and wondered if he should leave his
father. No pressure was applied to make him decide
either way and he eventually came with us. However,
he returned to his father the next day, as expected.
His father's cruelty and drinking could not break his
respect for him and like all travelling boys, he longed
for his father's respect in return. He considered that
the whole world had turned against his father, which
was not untrue, objectively speaking, and he could
not leave him in his hour of need. The other boys in
the camp discussed his action and considered it
foolish, but all would have done the same in the same
circumstances.

Need for affection

Outward signs of affection between parents and
children are rare except in the case of babies, and the
children tend to value any sign. John's children prized
a shilling each from their father on dole day (which
he gave them on Lizzie's return), and they did not
spend it that day but kept it to show the other
children, although they immediately spend anything
their aunts or uncles give them. Fatherly affection was
a sore point between John's children and Tom's. The
smugness of Tom's children, rich in fatherly affection,
angered John's deprived children and they watched

their father closely for appropriate times to be close
to him. All the children fought for maternal and
paternal affection and favours and for the very scarce
supply of possessions. When I took pictures of them,
fierce rivalry broke out between Winnie and Young
John for the pictures. I got copies and both were
happy but the next day Winnie's photographs were
gone. Although she had fought so hard for them, she
accepted this fatalistically, saying that you could not
have a thing with those children.

The presence of Bridget and her six extra
children was accepted without fuss but did pose
many problems. Teresa was depressed at the prospect
of the extra work the children would entail for her.
"It would be all right if their own mothers minded
them," she said. The new family were supposed to
live in a separate tent and be as self-sufficient as
possible. However, they moved into the main tent and
the two wagons of the main group, everyone moving
over and making room for them on the floor. They
contributed very little to the groceries. Bridget could
not beg in town in case she met her husband; and
the same applied to Cathleen, who did, however, go
to town to shop, and did some begging. Cathleen was
in charge of this family, taking absolutely no notice
of her mother's orders and showing open contempt
of her father. She had carried the burden of "finding"
for the family and minding the children for a long
time.

In the matter of food, the entire centre group now
dropped below any poverty line, the children eating
the scraps of the adults, who were eating the scraps
of the settled population. The children shared a cup
of tea between two or three and often had only dry
bread all day. Big Daddy ate very little anyway, but
now he simply stopped eating. There was only one
man with any regular income in the centre group—
Big Daddy, who was not expected to contribute his

money to the groceries. Francis did not get the dole. Mary had been paid £20 some time previously for handcrafts but was determined not to part with any of it.

The extended family offers support and practical help in difficulties but rarely financial assistance. In extreme cases the dependents will be fed but efforts will be made to ensure that they do not forget the need to support themselves. Big Mammy and Daddy were supporting two married daughters, a total of nine children, a single son and two single daughters, who, however, were more than supporting themselves.

The first week of the new family's stay was fraught with tension, between the women especially; the mothers were trying to secure a larger portion of the meagre rations for their own children, and the single girls were arguing over the work and Big Mammy was trying to lay down the law impartially. The men withdrew from the group, Big Daddy frequenting Tom's fire. Francis finally left at the end of the study and went to stay with his uncle who was making him a cart, which was a sign that he was to be married very shortly. Bridget and her children returned home after a week, due to the tension, but the children were back again two days later. Bridget stayed with her husband but came back to the camp sometimes.

The men collected sticks, attended to the horses and occasionally fetched water from springs. In John's case, Young John did most of these tasks and Francis did them for Big Daddy who, however, still collected sticks every day. They carried out repairs to wagons, tents, carts, etc. Tom made tin goods, both for the group and for sale.

The men all played a part in child-rearing, varying from helping with the practical tasks of washing and feeding, in Tom's case, to simply providing a model for them by their presence. Big Daddy exercised some control over all the children when he chose to exercise it but played a considerable part in the disciplining of Ann's sons. Francis, too, took part in disciplining the children when asked to do so. He paid attention to the fatherless children and provided some male identification for the boys, especially Young John. Like all Travellers, he felt great concern for the children and was in a better position to show it as his relationship with them all, that of uncle, was the same for all the children. He was not burdened with children of his own and had not the experience of being unable to provide adequately for children of his own. This inability can produce a lessening of interaction between father and children, as the father withdraws from the father-role so that he cannot be held responsible for failing in it. Francis showed more affection to the children than their fathers did, with the exception of Tom. He disapproved of their fathers' drinking and this caused many fights between him and John.

News and story-telling

In the evening, the men would relate the day's events, sometimes going back to their working days for stories. In the day's talking and gatherings, they kept up with the news of interest to them, news of jobs, deals, settlement committee ventures, "new inventions" and events in the outside world such as bank robberies. One might think that the women would perform the function of bringing back news of the settled world as they begged from it. This they did, but not in the same ritually-toned way the men did it. The men tended to seek a more equal relationship with settled people, and attempted to reduce the threat of the Garda by making a "friend" of him. They valued friendly relationships with settled people without ulterior motives of any kind, good or bad. Big Daddy was deeply hurt and humiliated by the behaviour of the local farmer. He passed up the road by the camp twice a day with his sons. The Wards had camped in the same place every winter for three years and the farmer had passed up and down for the same length of time but never even looked in their direction, pointedly ignoring their existence.

In a sense, the travelling man is the ambassador to the outside world, as opposed to the section of it dealt with by the women—the controlling and welfare agency sections. He spends a great deal of time sitting and watching, listening and talking. In a preliterate, self-entertaining society such as this, this function is extremely important. The woman is specifically prevented from having equal relationships with settled people by her dress and her begging function. Begging and equal relationships are incompatible.

Entertainment is poor most of the time, especially when they have no radios. Tom had an old radio which worked sporadically. My radio was very sought after by young and old alike. Story-telling, a very important entertainment, still exists but it appears to be dying rapidly and unlike the rest of rural Ireland, it has not been replaced with literacy for the Traveller. Solitary forms of entertainment are unknown. The ritual relaying of events by the men provides some entertainment, but they are not always present. Drinking, singing, dancing and talking are the traditional entertainment forms.

A match-making party

There was one party during my stay in the camp. It was a match-making party. Travellers have often told me that parties were much more common long ago. Perhaps the eye of the settled population is too much on the Travellers now to allow them to continue with their traditional self-entertaining. There was plenty of stout at the party; the children had their share and stayed up for it, of course. The party consisted of the newly-married couple from the wedding and a group of relatives, all men, including the match-maker for the area. Ann provided the music by "lilting". The men danced solitary reels, jigs and hornpipes with great solemnity and ritual. Then the single girls danced and finally men and women danced together. They all seemed to achieve a new dimension as each person displayed a talent and forgot the worries and difficulties of everyday life. They appeared to have an unbreakable solidarity, an illusion fostered by the men and silently disbelieved by the women. Ann's kinsmen assured her that they would murder her husband if they found him. Her only reply to their promises of a just revenge was "God is good, God is good."

During the singing and dancing the match-maker was sounding Mary's brother, Francis, and her brother-in-law, her sponsors who spoke for her, and the prospective husband about the match. The matter was very informal—the "throwing down of the match". Big Mammy was asked if she was satisfied and finally Mary was asked. She accepted reluctantly, knowing that she could change her mind before the final arrangements were made. No arrangements were made. It was difficult to discover what precisely had happened, but the match appeared to have been a hoax, a drunken joke with a serious message. All the men involved were kinsmen of Mary's. The parties have a traditional value, a value in the renewing of kinship ties which are very joyous occasions, and an entertainment value.

A Traveller is known to other Travellers by his tribe first and then by personal characteristics, often incorporated into his nickname. This is the same as the pattern in rural Ireland and rural societies gen-

erally. Status is ascribed, not achieved. Rivalry
between tribes is common and affects all areas of their
lives. The Travellers are person-orientated. The local
money-lender's tribe and the Wards had had many
disagreements before the man became a money-lender
at all. The money-lender was as illiterate as his clients
and no accounts were kept. He never stated the price
of an article, just the amount to be paid weekly or
monthly. Once a Traveller started doing business with
the money-lender he could hardly ever get out of his
grip, and he enforced payment with violence. The
money-lender sometimes descended on the Wards for
debts they had paid if the word got out that they had
got a sum of money from some source. Personal
animosity played a big part in the conduct of the
money-lender's business. It is difficult to say whether
many of his debts were ever paid, despite the violence.
Many of them certainly were, and many times over,
as he held a large number of the Children's Allowance
books in the area.

The outside world

Travellers speak of settled people as "the quality".
Their attitude towards "the quality" is often one of
fear. As previously mentioned, defensive beliefs
about settled people were common in the camp. Big
Tom was talking to a travelling boy who had just
left the local hospital about a little "quality" boy
that Tom had seen in the hospital when visiting. The
child had died and Tom questioned the Traveller
about the parents' reaction. When he heard that they
were calm and quiet, he said "You'd easily know
they weren't Travellers. Our hearts would be broke."
This was a common evaluation of settled people—
cold and hard-hearted, no doubt because this is how
we most often appear to them.

Travellers have a definite sense of inferiority

regarding "the quality". Of course, they divide settled
people into classes and prefer "the real quality"—
middle-class tolerant people—but Travellers who have
lived among working-class people for a while speak
highly of them. They are very much afraid of "teddy-
boys" whom they associate with the city, and this fear
appears to have foundation in some areas where they
are persecuted by gangs. They admire the dress and
possessions of settled people from a distance, sometimes condemning the dress as immoral. The majority
of Travellers, however, do not appear to be able to
imagine themselves in a similar position. In this sense,
they are truly traditional people, unable to imagine
anything other than what they are used to. This is
surprising in view of the existence of alternatives all
around them. They seem to feel that such things do
not apply to them and in their present conditions,
such alternatives have no practical meaning for them.
Yet some do succeed in making the change, such as
the three girls working in the hospital.

The institutions of the settled world have very
little relevance to the Travellers' lives and they do
not take part in them. Only three of the young people
ever went to Mass in the camp, yet I was expected
to go every Sunday. They are not disbelievers and are
not irreligious but they do not attend Mass for a
variety of reasons, the most common being shame of
their appearance, inferiority feelings, hostility of the
settled population, failure to understand the ceremony and lack of relevance to their lives. Priests are
generally highly respected but the Travellers are well
aware of their human faults and they are felt to be
too moralistic and punishing about the "action-seek-
ing" aspects of the Travellers' lives. Nuns are associ-
ated with schools and the attitude towards them is
much the same as towards priests, except they are
ranked lower in accordance with the general belief in
male superiority. Travellers feel ashamed about the

aspects of their lives disapproved of by the Church
but defensively justify them by their poor conditions.

Travellers do not vote. They are generally unaware
of the politics of the outside world, but Big Daddy
expressed an interest in the political news. However,
from his stories about "the Troubles", of which he
had many, it was clear that the fight was not theirs
and did not involve them. They gave shelter to both
sides, siding with the side who committed the least
atrocities at any one time, interpreting events in personal terms, horrified at the bloodshed caused by
fights based on ideals, unable to understand such an
abstract concept. They were aliens in their own land,
too closely bound to their struggle for existence to
appreciate fights based on ideology or ideals which
had no bearing on their lives as they saw it, and
would make no difference to their plight, one way
or the other. They are a voiceless minority, politically
powerless, and the effects of this powerlessness are
felt in their lack of control over their destinies, pro-
ducing loss of initiative and fatalism.

Travellers produce very little wealth and receive
very little in return. They work sporadically at
"settled" jobs. Economically, they often seem to be
trying to survive on the scraps and left-overs of settled
people. Many now receive the dole, but long periods
of dependence on the dole can be demoralising. Many
Travellers resent the fact that they are forbidden to
sell their tin cans or do other such business while
receiving the dole. Nevertheless, it is a great help and
in view of their living conditions, they do not receive
a disproportionate amount of welfare benefits.

Travellers are very deprived in the area of recreation. It was very noticeable that they could not go
into any of the cafes or restaurants in Galway. When
I was with the women, I was struck by the necessity to
be very submissive in relationships with settled people.
We stood back at bus stops and let "the quality" get

on first, bowed to the Gardaí, and refused to take offence or insults, as the following incident illustrates.

Returning home late one night from town, Big Mammy and Daddy, John and I were sitting on a crowded bus. All three Travellers were slightly intoxicated, especially Big Daddy who got drunk on three bottles of stout due to his eating habits. He sat beside a woman who was very drunk. She spoke to him and he responded in a friendly manner. Then she noticed that he was a tinker and started to insult tinkers in a loud voice. She said that she was a blacksmith's daughter and that the blacksmith refused to make the nail for the cross of Jesus but that the cursed tinker did. Big Daddy became very upset at this, which is a fairly common myth in rural Ireland and one which the Travellers are very sensitive about. He tried to argue with her but John and Big Mammy intervened, apologising for him. John, who has a very good voice, started to sing for the company. Big Mammy, in the meanwhile, cornered her husband and quietened him down. This had been a dangerous situation for them because Big Daddy, with his three bottles, had lost any accommodative attitude he had. Sometimes the women are unable to influence the men in this regard when they have been drinking. The man's accommodative attitude tends to be a thin cover for his real feelings, which he loses quickly when drunk. On the other hand, the woman's accommodative attitude is a deeply-ingrained part of her psychological being which she tends to retain even when drunk.

Fatalistic outlook

Almost every Traveller I spoke to had spent some time in hospital. Their health is bad and their living conditions so bad that they tend to be taken into hospital more frequently than settled people. Many Travellers have medical cards now though others still pay private doctors' fees. They like hospitals for the food, but are afraid of doctors, injections, operations. They have little faith in modern medicine or physicians, and are fatalistic about illness. The group studied had many tales to tell of receiving bad treatment or no treatment from doctors when they needed it. They have a great admiration for nurses and consider that they work too hard. This admiration is the direct result of close contact with nurses, as opposed to the doctors in the hospital. Hospital is a very lonely and frightening place for a Traveller, and his kin visit him often to mitigate his loneliness.

A favourite occupation of the older girls in the camp was counting the funerals coming out of the local hospitals. The numbers counted seemed to confirm their low opinion of the hospitals. Three Travellers, friends of the Wards, left a local hospital just before they were due to be operated on. Everyone agreed that it was a very foolish thing to do, but understood their feelings well.

Most of the Travellers in the camp could not count properly in our terms. Mary had only recently learned to count well. John often said: "I am the father of five children." In fact, he had nine children and three step-children. It is also important to note that many Travellers appear to have little or no idea of the relative value of money. Some Travellers speak in terms of fifty pounds, etc. in a way which clearly indicates that they do not know the value of large sums of money. Of course, they count and measure in their own terms, but in this area and many others, Travellers often use the "wrong" English word to express themselves. An example of this is the fact that Ann's property was always referred to as a "mare and a heifer" which led me to believe that Ann owned a cow. In fact, she owned two horses. I was unable to discover any reason for these "mistaken" references, of which there were many. Consequently, I noted that conversations between settled people and Travellers were sometimes completely at cross-purposes.

Travellers to date have participated only minimally in the educational institutions of the wider society. Their illiteracy is the measure of their isolation and deprivation. The desire for literacy in the camp I stayed in was strong. However, experience at school often causes Travellers to lose interest quickly. It is understandable that a teacher with a large class who has not got the time to find out about the Travellers' sub-cultural background will find them backward and tend to ignore them, making them feel stupid and so destroying their desire to learn. Sometimes the time spent at school will be very short. Travelling mothers sometimes have difficulty adjusting to the necessary changes in their lives when their older children go to school regularly. In practical terms this means that they must either stay at home with the younger children or take them with them everywhere. Aspirations are low but the majority of the young Travellers realise that they must be literate to get jobs.

Married with one child aged two years, PATRICIA MCCARTHY *has worked with Travellers in South County Dublin and North Wicklow for the past four years as a Social Worker employed by the Dublin Committee for Travelling People. Previous to this she did a socialised study of Travellers, resulting in a degree of Master of Social Science, from University College, Dublin in 1971.*

3 The Travelling People and Education

Some time ago I heard of two small travelling boys who had set fire to a National School because they had been refused places in it. I also heard an elderly Sister who had had travelling children in her classes for many years sum up her report on them in the words : "They're mad for education," and I heard another teacher say "The more you give them, the more they want."

What kind of education?

That the majority of the children of the travelling people want education, no one who is involved in trying to provide it for them would question. That they have a right to it in this nation of ours which has promised to cherish all its children equally, no one would deny. It is when we begin to consider the why, the what and the how of education that the problems begin to present themselves. Why do they need education? Education for what? What kind of education?

To study these questions, the Association of Teachers of the Travelling People (A.T.T.P.), was founded in 1972. It now has a membership of well over 200. We have no answers as yet, but one thing we are all agreed upon is that, unless the travelling people have some basic education, they will never really be free to make a choice between the life of the open road and the life of the settled community.

For generations they have lived on the fringe of society, tolerated by some, rejected and despised by many, accepted fully only by a few. Recently, for many reasons which are enlarged upon elsewhere in this book, they have come nearer to the settled community. Some of them have come right in out of the cold; others have made tentative steps towards integration; all have found the pressures of society coming to bear more and more heavily upon them. Education must help them to cope with these pressures, to survive in a world of cut-throat competition, and to preserve, if that is what they want to do, their own identity, their own culture, their own special strengths and their own special gifts.

And so those who are trying to provide education for them must build first on the rich inheritance that is already there. The travelling people have many strengths : the strong family bonds which unite them; the passionate loyalties which will often, in the school situation, make an older girl fight tooth and nail (literally!) for what she considers to be the rights of a young brother or sister; the unusual powers of physical endurance; the ability to live in and enjoy the present moment, however unhappy the background from which they have come that morning and to which they will be returning that evening.

The easiest way to tackle the problem of providing education for Travellers would undoubtedly be to send the school attendance officer to herd them into school, to wash them, brush their hair, tidy them up, tick their names in the register, make sure that they sit quietly in their desks during school hours—and hope for the best. But this would not be to provide education for them. They are *not* "just like other children", not because they are less clever (sample testing has shown that they can be as intelligent as any group of settled children), but because of the appalling social deprivation which they have suffered from earliest childhood.

The baby in a travelling family normally receives

the loving care of its mother just until the next baby
comes along (and generally that is within one year of
its birth), and after that it becomes the special charge
of one of the older children, often a child of not more
than seven or eight years. A travelling child is never
taught to speak—it picks up what it can from the
very limited vocabulary it hears used by the older
children and adults. The experience of a travelling
child, as compared with that of a child in the settled
community, is incredibly limited.

All these factors, and many more, mean that a
travelling child starts school, even if he starts at the
normal age (which is rare enough), severely handi-
capped. And so he needs very special attention, and
it is not always possible to provide this in the
ordinary class-room situation where a harassed
teacher may be trying to cope with the problems of
forty or fifty children from ordinary settled homes.

Education can open new worlds for the travelling
child. It can build up his self-confidence and give him
a self-respect which is often sadly lacking because of
the way in which society has treated him and his
people over the centuries. It can teach him to respect
others and to recognise that they have rights which
must be conceded to them. It can help him to improve immeasurably the quality of his life. But it
should not be geared to make the travelling child like
the rest of us, if that is not what the travelling people
themselves want. Many of them do, an increasing
number, perhaps, and if that is what they want, they
have a right to it. But the yardstick must always be
to provide for them the kind of education they need,
the kind of education which will make them free to
choose their way in life when they are old enough to
make a choice.

Until about ten years ago very few travelling
children ever attended school, apart from the few
weeks in early summer when they might go to the

local Convent to be prepared for First Communion and Confirmation. Now, in every part of the country, more and more of these children are attending National Schools with varying degrees of regularity, and emerging from them with a greater or lesser degree of literacy and numeracy.

Special needs

In order to understand something of these children's needs, it is necessary to look briefly at the background from which they set out for school. These backgrounds are as varied as the children themselves. Some travelling children come from families which have been housed for many years; some from recently housed families; some from families living in tigins on a properly serviced site; some from trailers, wagons or tents by the side of the road. And generally educational achievement follows the pattern of housing or settlement. This is not to say that the child from the housed family will always do better at school than the child from the roadside camp—we have seen many examples of children living in sub-human conditions by the side of the road getting themselves to school and doing remarkably well, even, in some few cases, in secondary school. Conversely, there are many examples of families well and comfortably housed who simply do not bother to send their children to school regularly. However, in general, poor living conditions result in poor school attendance and poor achievement.

This is not surprising. Just think what an achievement it is for a child living by the side of the road to come to school regularly, punctually and reasonably clean and tidy. She has often to get herself (and possibly her small brothers and sisters as well) out of the tent or wagon on a cold day, to find, if possible, some water in which to wash herself and them, and to set out for school often without even a hot cup of tea, because there is no means of lighting a fire at that time. Her parents will probably still be in bed, as they tend to go to bed very late, and this often means that the travelling children have also had a late, if not a disturbed, night. And so the child, wet and cold, hungry and often dirty, presents herself at the school door. And school is to her, at first anyway, a strange and frightening new world. Inevitably, if she is not welcomed with love and kindness, and more particularly if she is scolded for being late, or for not being clean, she will not persevere in her attempt to find out what school has to offer her.

The national school

Where the school is a good one, and there are many good ones, particularly in the small country towns of Ireland, the travelling child will be received with understanding, patience and love. Allowances will be made for the difficulties the child has to overcome to get to school at all, and in an accepting and caring atmosphere steady progress will be made.

In such a school one sees the benefits for the travelling child of education in an integrated class situation. The child who starts school at 4 or 5, attends regularly, and has reasonable support from home, however inadequate that home may be, will develop well, and often surpass in achievement the child from the settled community.

There is no lack of intelligence among the travelling children, and in a good school this will develop, and their many other talents, musical, artistic and creative, will appear. But when the travelling child starts late, and in a school where there is no special class, or no remedial teacher, and where big classes make it impossible for the teacher to give the child the necessary individual help, there is little hope of progress.

There are many cases of this up and down the country—travelling children sitting at the back of crowded class-rooms, their names ticked in the register, but learning little or nothing. As soon as they can, they will escape from the boredom and frustration of the situation, attendance will become spasmodic, and long before they have reached the required age, they will leave school, illiterate and having learnt little of value from their contact with the settled community.

On the whole, travelling children, probably because of their lack of confidence in themselves and their own abilities, are very easily discouraged, and fearful of making mistakes. Even where the school is a good and accepting one, these children start with grave disadvantages. They often come to school tired and upset by the happenings in the camp during the preceding night. Often there is little or no encouragement in the home, especially for the boys, to persevere with school. And often the girls are kept away to look after younger brothers or sisters.

Many travelling children have speech defects, and all of them suffer from the poverty of vocabulary which is the inevitable result of not having been taught to speak by a patient and concerned adult. It is worrying to go around the country and see the number of children who, even though they have had good and regular teaching, and have been coming to school for a considerable time, are still showing signs of appreciable retardation.

Irish Medical Association report

The recent report in the *Irish Medical Association Journal* on the deprivation of travelling children during the first year of life would go a long way towards explaining this disturbing fact. It gives details of a study of 95 infants from Travellers' families in Galway, and suggests that these children have smaller brains and weigh less than other infants as the result of disease and malnutrition, making clear that these deficiencies are caused by environment rather than heredity. The authors of the Report state : "It would be salutary if the opportunity to carry out further studies was denied to us by a rapid improvement in the habits and environment of these poor people. If these changes do not occur, it is possible that the continuation of adverse environmental and social features will lead to the perpetuation of a sub-culture with some limitation in brain size and intellectual capacity."

Commenting on this Report on the day it was published a leading article in *The Irish Times* stated : "Here, patently, is a group of children whose condition is remediable. Here, patently, is a group of people on the fringe of Irish society whose situation need not be perpetuated. Here, demonstrably, something can be done. Here, urgently, something must be done."

And what needs to be done urgently, and before the educational problem can be tackled with any hope of success, is to provide for the travelling families adequate living conditions where their children can grow up in reasonable standards of human comfort, well-fed, warm, properly clothed and with the possibility of keeping clean. It should not be difficult to do this, but the hard facts are that after nearly ten years of unremitting effort on the part of numerous Settlement Committees, there are still well over 600 families living on unauthorised sites, and many of them in sub-human conditions. There can be no real educational prospects for these children until something has been done about the background from which they come.

Special classes

Apart from the good work being done in many National Schools, and the less satisfactory conditions pertaining in others, there is a certain amount of special provision being made for the education of these children. Some of it is going on in the special classes attached to national schools, where travelling children are admitted on the understanding that they will progress from these to the ordinary classes. I know of one school which was completely successful in operating in this way. The children began in the special class, with an exceptionally enlightened and sympathetic teacher, and progressed into the normal classes with happy results and good integration.

But in general I would not be too happy with the arrangement; chiefly because it involves putting children of a wide age-group into the same class, and this is as bad for the children as it is for the teacher. No single teacher can cope with a class of twenty or so children aged from 5 to 12—particularly when these are travelling children with their very special needs and problems. Likewise no 10- or 11-year-old boy should be expected to start his education in the same class as his 5-year-old sister. It just does not work, and we have had ample proof that it is not the right approach.

Department of Education report

In 1970 the Department of Education brought out a *Report on Educational Facilities for the Children of Itinerants* in which it was stated that "the itinerant child has a right to expect the school system to attempt to meet his special needs". Unfortunately the Report went on to say that "the educational problems of itinerant children are similar in many respects to

those of backward children generally, aggravated by
social disabilities and a vagrant way of life".

The apparent backwardness of the travelling child
is one of the many by-products of social deprivation,
and the remedy must lie first in the area of social welfare, and the effort to compensate for the many disadvantages which prevent the travelling child from
progressing according to his or her natural ability.
This cannot be done either in the overcrowded classes
of many of our national schools, or even in the
"special class" situation where a teacher, often with
no particular qualifications for the task, is trying to
cope with a group of 5- to 12-year-olds, each of whom
needs an enormous amount of individual attention
and personal care.

A social problem

As Dr Cyril White said when he addressed the
first National Conference of the Association of
Teachers of the Travelling People in September 1972,
"The whole problem is not strictly an educational
one, but rather a social problem with educational im-
plications." That is why many people who are involved in the education of travelling children feel
that, at any rate for those families who are still not
settled, but living by the side of the road, very special
facilities are needed if education is ever going to
achieve anything worthwhile for them. Where there
are two or more special classes attached to national
schools, good results can be and are sometimes
achieved, because here it is not necessary to put
children of widely differing age-groups into the same
class; and under the guidance of enlightened teachers
much can be done to help the travelling child to
develop and to integrate with the children in the
other classes in the school.

Special schools

In two or three places in Dublin, and in one in Limerick, there are examples of such "schools within a school", where the real problems and needs of these children are recognised and catered for, and excellent work is being done. There is also in Dublin one special school for travelling children, situated on a large camp site and drawing its children solely from the families on that site. This school is the *only* special school for travelling children recognised and financed by the Department of Education.

No account is taken of the situation where there is a large number of families fairly permanently camped in a particular area, but not on *approved* sites, and therefore subject to constant "moving on" at the request of local residents. Such a situation pertains in South County Dublin where 53 families have been camped for a number of years. None of these families have been settled by the local authorities, and since many of them are continually harassed by local residents and others, there would be little chance of education for any of their children were it not for the existence of a special school for travelling children in Old Connaught Avenue, Bray.

St Kieran's School

St Kieran's is a special school for Travellers and is supported largely by contributions from well-wishers and friends. It has received in the past a Department of Education grant amounting to just over one-third of its running costs, because official Department policy has been that such schools are not needed for travelling children. But it is an incontrovertible fact that the children attending St Kieran's (there were 121 on the rolls last term) would not be receiving any education at all if the school were not there to provide it.

As this is in many ways a unique experiment in the education of travelling children, I would like to describe what goes on in it in a little more detail.

Pre-school classes

There are five classes in the school, and the first two are pre-school classes, for children between the ages of three and six. When the school was first started four years ago the under-fives were not taken until it was discovered that the older pupils were being kept at home to mind the little ones, so that the only way to get them to school was to let the little ones come too; and secondly that it was essential anyway for these very deprived children to get the help they needed as early as possible.

The two teachers in these classes are Montessori trained, and this method is particularly suited to the children in the younger classes. Anyone who thinks that Montessori is a middle-class approach to education should come and visit St Kieran's.

The first thing the children have to learn when they come to school is that adults from the settled community, their teachers, are people they can trust, people who care for them, people of whom they need never feel afraid. Fear and distrust are the immediate reactions of the travelling children to adults from the settled community, and until this has been eradicated and a good personal relationship established with the teacher, very little can be done. Even here the teacher is faced with immediate problems—the child will often be so shy and inarticulate that even the effort to give his name may take quite a lot of time and patience. Often too, he will find the teacher's way of speaking, so different from that of his mother at home, very difficult to understand.

So there are communication barriers to be broken down from the word "go", but unless this is achieved the child may well take a dislike to school, or such a fear of it that it will be difficult to get him ever to return. Having established a degree of trust and confidence in the child, the teacher will then help him to gain a knowledge of, and control over, his environment through the use of materials such as water, sand, paint, etc.

A great deal of time is spent during the first months (or even longer) in teaching the children how to play, as they have had no toys at home and have never really played. So the pre-school class-rooms contain many toys, a "house corner" where they can for the first time "play house", as well as the water, sand and paint they will soon come to need. And since they often come to school in the morning in a highly disturbed state of mind after a family fight in the camp, perhaps, or a drinking bout among the adult population, the teacher must be able to provide for them a calm and ordered environment, in which tensions can be relaxed and tranquillity restored.

In the "house corner" a child can often be seen acting out her particular fears and anxieties, and here too she learns a lot about "social behaviour". It is a real treat to be invited to a cup of tea by some small girls in the "house corner", and to see their total absorption in pouring out the imaginary tea and milk and spooning in the imaginary sugar, while all the time entertaining you with a steady flow of comment on what is going on.

Learning to communicate with the teacher through stories and conversation is the next essential step in their progress, and the more they can be helped to talk, and so to increase their very meagre vocabulary, the more ready they are going to be for later steps in reading and writing.

Music and art also play an important part in the education of these pre-school children. Music played softly in the background has a very soothing effect on a disturbed child, and singing is something for which travelling children have a rare talent, and one which should be more fully explored. Artistically, we have found them exceptionally gifted. Through painting they can learn to express themselves, and it is important that they be allowed to paint as they like— which at first means covering a great deal of paper with a great deal of paint. But soon patterns begin to emerge, and it is not long before the outlines of wagons, horses, and dogs are beginning to appear on the paper. They have a rich sense of colour, and love to express this in their paintings.

I always notice with joy in the pre-school classes the gradual dawning of the ability to concentrate. On the whole travelling children find concentration very difficult—in many cases it seems to be almost impossible at first. But gradually, as different materials are presented to them, and they learn how to control a brush or pencil, they reach a stage where you find them so absorbed in what they are doing that nothing seems able to distract them. One day last year I had a photographer in one of the pre-school classrooms for a whole morning, and she was amazed at the way in which the children were so absorbed in what they were doing that they paid not the slightest attention even to the flashing of her bulb as she took close-ups of their intent little faces.

The Montessori system

One aspect of the Montessori system which is particularly helpful to travelling children is the encouragement of independence and initiative. The teacher "helps the child to help himself" while being careful to avoid giving any unnecessary help to him. Mutual aid takes the place of competition and the children help each other—especially where older children can help younger ones, as happened recently in St

Kieran's when a small boy (Puss) offered to help a young sister (Womans—the names are intriguing) to write her name, and the offer was accepted!

Another helpful aspect of the Montessori system is the encouragement of spontaneous self-discipline. Travelling children have a great need of the freedom which comes from being in control of themselves and of their environment. It is so often drummed into them at home that they have to fight for their "rights", and to get their maximum share of everything going (including the undivided attention of the teacher), that their immediate reaction to almost anything, even the distribution of biscuits, is to try and get there first and make sure of their share—until they have learnt to trust the distributing adult enough to know that fair shares will be had by all! This means an aggressiveness and an instant resort to violence on the least provocation, which can only be counteracted by the inculcation of self-discipline. School has to show them that it is not necessary to fight for things in an atmosphere where everyone is going to be equally cared for, and also that other people have rights too, and these must be respected.

The older classes

All these lessons, and many more, begin in the pre-school classes, and are continued and added to as the children go up the school. In the three top classes of St Kieran's a much wider programme of education is offered to the children. There is, of course, a certain concentration on helping them to become literate and numerate, but other doors are opened as well. Religious instruction is an essential part of the curriculum, and one which is more highly valued than any other subject by the majority of the parents. In the early days of the school parents felt not enough time was being given to "teaching the children their prayers", this being the principal reason for sending them to school in the first place. One of the main concerns of the teachers, on the other hand, is to help the children to disentangle the superstitions in their religion from the real and deep faith which underlies them.

Then the teachers try to open for them as many doors as possible onto the rich inheritance of the world around them—nature study, legends, simple history and geography, art, music and drama. The school has been fortunate in having the voluntary contribution of a visiting art teacher for the last few years, and this supplements the daily excursions into the field of painting and crafts which goes on in the class-rooms. In drama, too, the school has been very fortunate, as the Young Abbey Players have paid a weekly visit to the school to do creative drama with the older children.

And then of course there are the school outings, which are among the most enriching experiences of the children: the annual visit to the Peacock Theatre to see *The Golden Apple* or *The Golden Horseshoe*, when they sit enthralled by what is going on on the stage, with that total "suspension of disbelief" of which only children can be really capable; the annual visit to the Zoo which provides them with topics for conversation and for writing about for weeks afterwards; visits to the Horse Show, the Spring Show, the Rosc Exhibition and so on. And then, the crowning experience of every school year, the week at Ballymoney, when they live in a real house (lent by a member of the Committee), sleep in real beds, wear real night clothes, swimsuits, etc., and spend blissful days in and out of the water and playing on the sandy beach. This is a week rich in experience for teachers as well as pupils, and new bonds of friendship and understanding are formed which could never develop simply in the school situation.

Disadvantages of a special school

Although a special school can do so much for travelling children, it has its disadvantages. There is inevitably an element of segregation in it—all the children are travelling children, although, unlike the special school on a camp site, they are children from a wide variety of families camped in a fairly wide-spread area. The school minibus which collects them for school each morning does about 500 miles a week on its rounds. Another disadvantage is that a group of disturbed travelling children in a school like this, or even one disturbed child in a class, can disrupt the whole atmosphere of the school or class, and this would be less likely to happen in an ordinary class in an ordinary school. Also, the children are not able to learn from the children of the settled community as they could in an ordinary school, or, for that matter, to contribute their own special strengths to the children in the ordinary school. A special school may not be the best answer, but it is certainly a "better than nothing" one.

The role of the parents

A very important element in the whole field of education for travelling children is the part played by the parents. Increasingly, the travelling parents are looking for education for their children. Their ideas about what education is may be limited—for most of them it is confined to the basic skills of reading, writing and preparation for the Sacraments. For a long time the child's confirmation day marked the end of his school attendance, but increasingly they are prepared to leave them longer at school if they think they are gaining anything from it.

But there are still many parents who set no store whatever by education, and these are, on the whole, the more well-to-do Travellers, or those who are living in such sub-human conditions that the effort to get children to school is just beyond them. The philosophy of the well-to-do travelling parents is that they have got on very well themselves without being able to read and write, and they see no need to send their children to school, apart from the necessity to have them prepared for Holy Communion and Confirmation.

These parents are as badly in need of education as their children, and I think that one of the ways in which a special school can help is by having parents' meetings, where the parents can come and meet the teachers, see their children's work, and make their criticisms known. These meetings can be a good way of educating parents about certain values, religious and otherwise, which the teachers are trying to inculcate in their children. A good relationship between teachers and parents is essential if the children are going to be allowed to attend school regularly and make good progress. It is very noticeable in different parts of the country that the best results are always achieved where some concerned teacher is visiting the families outside school, and has some knowledge of their particular problems.

The teenagers

From the parents, we might turn for a minute to the teenagers. From the educational, social and moral point of view, the travelling teenager is perhaps the one presenting most problems and in most urgent need of help. In the survey I am at present making, I have found only a handful of teenagers, so far, who are literate, or prepared in any way to earn a living. This is particularly true of the boys, but the girls too show a high percentage of illiteracy, and even when they have been attending a national school regularly the picture is nearly always one of early leaving, and back to the camp, to begging, to early marriage.

In many parts of the country splendid efforts are being made to provide some basic education and leisure activities for teenage Travellers, mostly by voluntary committees or organisations. In Dublin there are now three full-time youth leaders doing an excellent job in the big camp sites. In Athlone an exciting Night School is catering on three nights of the week for young Travellers who want to learn to read and write, to cook, to do woodwork, to play an instrument, or simply to play table-tennis or other games. In Bray, a night school operates twice a week to teach illiterate teenagers to read and write. In many other places, voluntary teachers or other concerned people are trying to do what they can for these young people.

One of the disquieting aspects of the situation is that many of the teenagers who come to these classes have spent longer or shorter periods in national schools, and emerged illiterate. This should improve as more travelling children are going earlier to school, attending more regularly, and having the benefit of special education or remedial teachers who are now on the staffs of an increasing number of schools. But it will be years before the problem is solved, and as time is passing for these teenagers it is imperative to see that they get all they can before it is too late.

And I do not mean simply that their right to literacy be recognised and catered for. There are other needs which we should also be trying to meet. Young Travellers need a great deal of education in the matter of sex and marriage. Most of their marriages are still "arranged" for them by their parents, and in some cases the young people meet for the first time on their wedding-day or just before.

Many of the marriages are of young people far too

young to be taking on the responsibilities of marriage.
Recently I was talking to a young travelling woman
who had got married at the age of thirteen and
had 26 children before she was forty. Many of
these marriages are loveless from the start, and the
young people enter into them without any understanding of what marriage is going to demand of
them. Here a whole programme of education for our
travelling teenagers is needed. So also do they need to
know about the dangers of alcoholism or heavy drinking before they have formed a habit of it which they
cannot easily break. And for the girls there should be
courses in child care, hygiene, cookery, buying, home-
making, etc.

Priorities

As we survey the whole field of education for the
travelling people and see what has been done, is being
done, and could be done, certain priority areas
emerge.

First there is a great need for pre-school classes,
where travelling children of 3 and 4 years of age can
receive the compensatory education which makes it
possible for them to enter ordinary schools at the
right age, less disadvantaged than the majority of
them are at present. This is a need which should be
met not only for travelling children, but for many
other children who are deprived, for one reason or
another, in early childhood. It could well be ideal for
such classes to contain both children from the settled
community and travelling children.

There is a need for pre-school classes of a different
kind—classes into which travelling children of 5 years
and over, who have missed out on early education, can
go to be prepared for entry into national schools if
their parents desire this.

Then there is a need for special classes for travel-

ling children of 7, 8, 9 and upwards, who are so far
behind their own age-group that no amount of special
help could ever enable them to join an ordinary
class. These classes should not be for widely ranging
age-groups, but the younger children should be in one
class and the older in another. Teachers in these
classes should have special training for what is a very
specialised form of teaching. These classes would also
cater for families who are still by the side of the road,
and are therefore unable, for social or other reasons,
to join ordinary schools. Where there are large numbers of families of this kind in any one area, a special
school may be necessary. In this, as in the classes
mentioned above, the policy should be that wherever
the parents want it, the children will be prepared for
entry into the national schools. But one has to recognise that many of the national schools have in fact no
room for these children, even if they presented themselves for enrolment.

Within the schools themselves there is a great
need for more remedial teachers, and where a school
is opening its doors to a large number of travelling
children, it should be given priority in the allotment
of a remedial teacher, or a special education teacher.
Also, in the schools there should be a degree of understanding of the odds against which many travelling
children are fighting in order to get themselves to
school, and a resulting degree of tolerance of any lack
of punctuality or cleanliness which may result from
this.

Apart from the teachers, the key people in education for travelling children are the social workers, who
can do so much to help teachers to understand
Travellers, and so much to help parents to value
what the school has to offer their children. There
should therefore be a very close liaison between the
social worker and the school authorities as at St
Kieran's, for example, where the social worker attends

all staff meetings, and makes an invaluable contribution to the discussions.

For the teenagers we need more classes to help them to become literate, and for this many more voluntary teachers must be found, because far and away the best method of teaching a teenage Traveller is on a one-to-one pupil-teacher basis. We also need more Youth Leaders in many areas of the country, to help the young Traveller to keep out of trouble, to fulfil himself by learning new ways of enjoying life and new ways of earning a living. At a recent meeting of the Association of Teachers of the Travelling People, the many problems of the teenage Traveller were discussed under the heading of employment, leisure, delinquency, literacy and alcoholism. The deep concern expressed for these young people by many members of the conference highlighted the urgency of the need to find ways of helping them—before it is too late.

Although the need for teachers, social workers and youth workers is paramount, much can be done (and indeed much has already been done) by members of the settled community who care enough to want to help these young people. One of the most encouraging developments of the last twelve months has been the formation of the H.O.T. (Helpers of Travellers) Groups in the senior classes of post-primary schools. The first objective of this group is "To break down prejudice against Travellers in the settled community", and if anyone can accomplish that task it will certainly be the young people of the country. They are totally devoid of prejudice themselves, and find it difficult to understand it when they see it in their elders. They have already organised integrated parties, dances and ceilis for groups of travelling teenagers, and they seem to be able to relate to them without any barriers. Another group which has come into being recently is the "Travellers Action Society", in Trinity College, Dublin. Their work is with travelling children, young mothers and wives. There is hope for the future of education for travelling people when groups of young people like these are concerned enough to take action.

Delegation to Holland

In September 1972 I had the privilege of going to Holland with a Delegation from Ireland to study the efforts of the Dutch Government at settling and educating the 35,000 travelling people in their country. (Holland has a similar problem to our own in that all its Travellers are native Dutch people, just as ours are all Irish.)

In 1970 a new *Caravans Act* was passed in Holland. It provides for nursery and primary education for the children on the sites; social work for the individual, family and group; health care, and moral and spiritual welfare. A typical site in Holland would have anything up to 120 families on it, and their caravans are incredibly opulent—deep carpets, beautiful ornaments, TV, deep freeze and so on. Most of the ones we visited had more than one bedroom, as well as a large living-room. They are so beautiful, and the Dutch Travellers so house-proud, that the children are never allowed to play inside them. If it rains (as it does very often in Holland) they have to stay outside—and play *under* the caravans!

On every site there is an extensive social centre, with large recreation rooms, bar, cafeteria, chapel, medical room, creche for the babies and so on. There is also, on every site, a magnificent school, complete with gymnasium, home economics room, workshops for the boys, etc. The schools are of a standard which would compare favourably with any in the world. They are bright and airy, very well-equipped, and staffed by a generous number of dedicated teachers.

The pupil-teacher ratio is one to fifteen in these schools, but very seldom did we see a class with as many as fifteen children in it.

The courses followed are similar to those in the ordinary national schools, and all the same books, equipment, etc. are provided. There are 48 such special schools for Travellers' children in Holland, with 240 full-time teachers, 86 of them for the under-sixes. The standard of work in the schools is excellent. Nearly all the children read and write fluently, and some are well above average, but though many of them had been in school for seven or eight years, there were few examples of any of them going on to further education, and in one school where the head-mistress said she had the children of mothers who had been at school there in their time, we found that the mothers had, on leaving school, simply gone straight back to the camp.

In 1964 the Government was uneasy about the apparently "disintegrating effect of the schools on the caravan-dwellers' community" and the Secretary for Education and Science requested the Pedagogics Institute of the State University of Utrecht to undertake a qualitative study of the functioning of the schools. The study revealed, among other things, that the percentage of educationally sub-normal children was no higher than the corresponding percentage for the population as a whole, but that there was a wide development lag in these children. The University of Utrecht then devised an enrichment programme to compensate for this.

They found that the strong hostility of the caravan-dwellers to the settled community (and *vice versa*) which has built up through years of discrimination, carries over into the work of education, and the teachers are still regarded by the parents as representatives of the settled population. The parents do not set a very high value on education, and there is consequently a certain discrepancy between the two environments of home and school. Also it has been found that parents give little attention to their older children, are not consistent in their upbringing, are too permissive with them, rarely or never play with them, and make no contribution whatever to their language development. All this sounds very like the problems we have in Ireland. The "enrichment programme" is intended for the older nursery school children, and is aimed at helping these children to close the development gap which is the result of the environment in which they live. It constitutes a systematic preparation for primary school, and as such is an essential supplement to the existing work-and-play methods used in the nursery school.

We came away from Holland very impressed by the genuine efforts of the Dutch Government to try to find a solution to their problem. They have spent millions of pounds on the Travellers, have provided magnificent facilities, and are really anxious to do the best they can for the travelling people of Holland. And yet we felt that we in Ireland must look for solutions along a different path.

In Holland, too much money has been spent, too much has been provided, and the result is that the camps are in effect ghettos. Situated well off the beautiful roads which traverse the country, they are so provided with everything they need, that there is no incentive for the Travellers to move into the often hostile world of the settled community. Although the children in the schools were reaching such a good academic standard, only a very small proportion were showing any inclination to work in the settled community after leaving school.

Mr John Wondergem, from the Ministry of Culture, Recreation and Social Work, voiced the unease of many Dutch officials who are engaged in working for the Travellers in Holland when he said:

"We have followed *our* aims. Did we ask them were they *their* aims too? We must start where they are. We must accept them without reservations, accepting that there are differences, and there will remain differences between them and us. We have to realise that they have a right to be a group. We must make it clear that we are not just trying to get rid of them in a nice place which is a ghetto."

These are wise words, and echo the ideas which must always lie behind our thinking about the right kind of education for travelling people. No one way is the right way. The Travellers are all very different from one another in spite of the strong bonds which unite them as an ethnic group, and their needs are as diverse as themselves, and must be met as diversely. They differ in the degree of their aspiration for settlement, and in the kind of education they need and want. Our task is to seek to assess, with them, the nature of that need and desire, and to do our best to provide for it, keeping ever in mind that education is for freedom, the freedom to be what they want to be, what God made them to be, the freedom to answer or to reject the call of the road, the freedom to be fully themselves.

SISTER COLETTE DWYER *was born in 1917 in Cork. She joined the Society of the Holy Child, took her M.A. in English at Oxford and was Headmistress in England for 17 years. Manager of St Kieran's School for Travelling Children, which she founded in 1969, she is now National Coordinator for the Education of Travellers.*

4 Settlement of the Travelling People

The last five or six years have brought about an amazing change in the lives of a great number of the travelling people. Approximately 800 families out of the total 1,450 in the country are now living in permanent or semi-permanent conditions, either in houses, pre-fabs or in trailers on authorised sites. These people have looked for and accepted settlement. No compulsion has been used to induce them to settle. They have done so because they wished to.

Slow beginnings

The Report of the Government Commission on Itincrancy was published in 1963, but from then until about 1969 progress in settlement was slow, painful and haphazard. By that time, the various local Voluntary Committees were using every means in their power to highlight the wretched living conditions of the Travellers in their areas. They were urging their Local Authorities to implement the recommendations of the Government Commission, while at the same time doing all they could to bring about a greater spirit of tolerance and sympathy in the hearts of the settled community. Needless to say, neither of these was an easy task. While the Local Authority officials might have been willing enough to provide accommodation for the Travellers, the settled community, and through them, the elected representatives, objected strenuously to the whole idea.

This was understandable, of course. Up till then,

very few people really knew "the tinkers". They were
feared—or despised—because of their anti-social
habits, their wild appearance and their dirty encamp-
ments. Very few people really believed that the vast
majority of the Travellers now wanted to settle down.
Even if they did believe it, the idea that the travelling people had a *right* to a settled home, if they
wanted one, was something too revolutionary to be
entertained. And when at last it became obvious
that they had both the desire and the right to settlement, most people were horrified by the prospect of
having a "tinker family" housed anywhere near them.

Changed situation

Yet now, five years later, the situation is greatly
changed. They have been years of effort and frustration, hope and disappointment, courage and perse-
verance on the part of those who were engaged in the
settlement programme. They have been years of
disbelief, suspicion or hostility on the part of a large
section of the settled community. Nevertheless, the
change has taken place. The settlement movement is
under way, and acceptance of it is growing steadily
throughout the country.

Most people have begun to realise that the
settlement of the Travellers is not an impossibility;
and that, given the chance, they do not make such
bad neighbours after all. They have also begun to
see that it is not alone in the Travellers' interests that
they should be settled; it is also in the interests of
the settled community that we should remove forever
from the face of our lovely country the stigma of the
inhuman conditions of those filthy and wretched
roadside camps.

About 400 travelling families have been housed
during the past six years in standard houses. Over
200 are now living, either singly or in groups, in

prefabricated dwellings on official sites. About 150 families have been given trailers or mobile homes on authorised, serviced sites. And a new spirit of cooperation has evolved between the Local Authority officials and the Settlement Committees.

Mistakes inevitable

During the long process of experimentation in the various forms of accommodation to be provided for the travelling people, it was inevitable that mistakes be made. There was no blue-print for the successful settlement of this underprivileged group, and consequently different areas tried different methods, with varying degrees of success or failure. So many people —both official and voluntary—thought they knew exactly what was needed, and so many people have been proved wrong. But these mistakes should not discourage us; they can, in most cases, be rectified, and we can learn from them. Above all, they have taught us our greatest, basic lesson. That is, that all Travellers are not the same; that what is right for one family may not necessarily be right for the next; that we must spare no effort in finding out what *they* want, before presuming to decide what their needs are; that we must, in fact, get to know them.

All Travellers are not the same

The travelling people are as rich in variation as any other section of our Irish people. While they may share one common attribute—their underprivileged background—they vary individually as much as any of us, in their personalities, their potential abilities, their strengths and weaknesses. That is why it has proved so unwise to generalise about them. However, with caution, it may be possible at this stage of our experience to divide them loosely into

four main categories, when it comes to deciding what
type of accommodation should be provided for them
at any one point in time. (I use the words "at any one
point in time" advisedly, because again, like all of
us, the Travellers change, adapt and develop in every
new situation.) Tentatively then, I would divide them
into the following categories:

1. Those families who wish to give up their old
   way of life, to settle down in ordinary houses
   and to integrate fully with the settled population.
2. Those families who would like to settle down, but
   who still want to retain their own identity as a
   group, and do not desire complete integration
   with the settled community.
3. Those families who would like the security of a
   settled place to live, but are as yet too fearful
   to commit themselves to the unknown stresses of
   coping with a house.
4. Those families who do not wish to settle in any
   one place, but want to continue their wandering
   way of life but in a way that befits a human
   being.

In order to be sure about these categories, it is
very important that those of us who are engaged in
the settlement programme should try to get to know
each individual family on a personal basis. It is
essential, so as to avoid mistakes, that we find out
what the family really wants, and not be guided by
what we, the settled community, would like them to
want!

It may well be that many people will think that all
this categorising is unnecessary. They might argue
that trying to suit each individual family's taste is just
so much sentimental theorising; and anyway, in their
opinion, the families should just take what they are

given, and be thankful. I disagree, for two reasons.

First, from a psychological point of view, why should anyone take what he is given and be thankful, if it is not what he wants? Would you or I go and live in a palace, if all we wanted was a small country cottage? Would we accept a two-roomed flat, if we needed a two-storied house? Would we settle down among strangers, in a strange country, if there was any possibility of getting a house where we wanted it, among our own people in Ireland?

Secondly, on a practical level, if the family does not like the accommodation it is given, it will leave and go back on the road. That particular attempt at settlement will have been a failure, and we will all be "back to square one".

Consequently, I would stress again the need to study each individual family's needs and aspirations before deciding on what kind of accommodation should be provided. Voluntary workers are naturally in a better position to do this than the officials are. That is why it is so important that a close liaison be maintained between the voluntary groups and the Local Authorities. It is encouraging to note that this cooperation has been growing over the past few years. Not alone have the authorities become more willing to accept responsibility for providing accommodation for the Travellers, they have also become more willing to consult with the workers in the field, who know the families. Because of this, some remarkably successful settlement has been achieved.

Houses

Let us look first at the progress so far in the provision of standard housing for Travellers. About 400 ordinary houses have been allocated to travelling families during the last six years. Some are in new housing estates, some in older terrace houses, some in County Council cottages, etc. I have visited scores of these newly-housed families during the last year in every part of Ireland. In the majority of cases, their adaptation to their new environment has been excellent. But not in all cases. There are some who are not suited to this kind of housing, who are unable to cope, who are unhappy and who will probably leave the houses and return to the roads before very long.

There are far more, however, who are settling down happily in their new homes. These are the ones who really want houses; they were given the kind of housing they applied for, and they are satisfied. Neither they nor their children will ever go back on the roads again, unless they are forced to go. Sometimes at first, some of them are nervous of their neighbours and anxious about their ability to cope with the new situation. This is where they can be helped tremendously by the supportive after-care of the Committee members and/or Social Workers, where they are available.

How often have I wished, when visiting these newly-housed families, that the cynics could be there with me too, to see for themselves. I'd like them to see the well-furnished houses, the warm and tidy kitchens, the painting and tiling which they so often do themselves, the children doing homework at the table, the whole family gathered round the television at night. I'd like them, too, to see the joy which simple amenities like dry clothes, a running tap, a warm bed or a bath can give the families. As one young father told me a few weeks after he'd moved into a new house in a modern estate, "Nothing will persuade me to give up this house. I've waited ten years for it. I'll pay my rent and be as good as anyone else. I want to be able to talk to the man in the house next door, and maybe go for a drink with him of an evening. I want my wife to talk to his wife. I want my kids to forget they were ever called tinkers."

Other families feel the same, although they may not be so articulate. Mr and Mrs A, and their fifteen children, live now in a County Council cottage, a mile outside a country town. They have been there for two years, and the garden is full of potatoes and vegetables. They are well-known and liked by the settled neighbours, as they camped regularly in the area for many years before they were housed. The father and eldest son deal in scrap, and keep it neatly piled and sorted behind the house. One son is in the Army and is going to marry a girl from the settled community. Two of the older daughters cycle to work every day to a local factory; the younger children attend the local national school.

It is always a help if the family is already known in the locality, as it eases the tension which may arise when the settled people realise a travelling family is about to be housed in their midst. Yet many of the families are not so fortunate, and may have to contend with a good deal of hostility from the neighbours when they first move in. Mr and Mrs B were like that.

This couple were in their sixties when I first met them. They lived in a canvas tent on the roadside; their large family had all grown up and gone away. Mr B had tuberculosis and because of this, he and his wife were eventually given a ground floor Corporation flat. At first, the neighbours across the landing were terrified of them, and did everything they could to get them evicted. They bolted all their doors and windows at night in case of assault or rape. The mother complained bitterly—to officials, Social Workers and Committee members—that she would have a nervous breakdown if the "tinkers" were not put out. Yet now, after eight months, that settled woman says: "You couldn't have nicer neighbours. We're the best of friends and I often drop over for a chat."

I could give many other examples like that, of successful housing and integration. In all cases, it applies to those families who fall into the first category I mentioned: those who really want it. But the picture unfortunately would not be complete if I did not mention also the many cases where standard housing and integration have been offered to families in the other three categories, that have *not* been successful.

I have found many who have discovered, to their disappointment, that living in a house in a settled neighbourhood was just not what they had expected. They feel lonely for their old travelling companions; they feel isolated and ill-at-ease among people who do not understand them or make allowances for their shortcomings. The mother is unable to cope with the housekeeping, budgeting, time-keeping and all the other chores which are completely new to her. Things which come naturally to most of us, like speaking quietly, dressing in a certain way, keeping the garden tidy and the front door shut, are all quite difficult for the Travellers. At this stage, they really cannot "keep up with the Joneses" in the settled community. They feel inferior, ostracised and isolated in their new surroundings. Many of them, after a valiant attempt to settle, will eventually find they can stick it no longer, and they will return to the roadside.

Direct housing, in these cases, has been a mistake, due to hasty or unsound assessment on the part of the housing authorities or voluntary workers. Sometimes, those families who do not succeed in settling the first time will come back later and try again; and perhaps the next time they will succeed. But for their first attempt, it would have been better to give them a chalet, rather than a standard house.

Chalets

Chalet is the name given to the small, prefabricated dwellings which are being erected in groups for the Travellers by many Local Authorities. They are particularly suitable for those families whom I have mentioned in my second category: those who wish to retain their own identity as a group and do not desire complete integration with the settled community. Chalets are useful, too, of course, for providing a quick method of accommodating temporarily those in the first category: those who want eventually to be housed in a standard house, but for whom no house is available. As long as they are not kept waiting too long, a short stay on a chalet-site can be a useful preparation for standard housing.

The chalets are usually erected in groups, where a number of families are enabled to live together on the same site, among their own people. Here they do not experience the feelings of isolation or inferiority which they might do if they were given a house in the settled community. There are not the same pressures on them to change their old life-style. Scrap-dealing and the keeping of horses—both legitimate activities—are still permissible, if the site has been properly planned to include them.

At the same time, they can experience their first taste of settled living, amid comfortable surroundings. Inevitably the basic amenities which they now enjoy in the chalet will appeal to the majority, and this situation frequently acts as an initial encouragement to them to keep and value a settled home. After a year or two in a chalet, it has often been found that a family who at first had no wish for a standard house among settled neighbours will now decide to apply for one. Others will wish to remain. In either case, the chalet is serving a useful purpose.

Chalets sites are now to be seen in many parts of

the country, Almost 300 units have been erected in the last six years, in groups varying from 39 in Labré Park, Dublin, to 22 in Dundalk's St Helena's Park, to 12 in Shinrone's Milltown Park, or 2 in Tullamore. The new Cara Park site at Coolock, Co. Dublin, is a fine example of how far the chalets have come on, in design and size, since the very first ones were erected in Labré Park in 1967.

At that time they were known as "tigins". They were simple, one-roomed prefabs, each one including a toilet, wash-basin and solid-fuel stove. They were designed on the assumption that the families would use them merely as living quarters, while keeping their caravans alongside for sleeping accommodation. It was soon discovered, however, that most of the families tended also to sleep in the tigins, since they were warmer, and the caravans tended to be used less and less.

Naturally then, subsequent provision of tigins has tended towards larger and more spacious dwellings, to provide for sleeping as well as living. They are now so like standard houses that we have dropped the name "tigins" (except in referring to the original, one-roomed variety) and, for want of a better name, we are using the word "chalet" to indicate the kind of structure which is now being provided. Many of the old tigins are still in existence. They have served their purpose well, and still suit many of the families living in them. But as each year passes, the design is being changed and adapted, in line with further experience. First a bedroom was added, then two, then three. A proper bathroom is now an essential and it is considered inadequate to provide anything less than three bedrooms for a mixed family of parents, boys and girls.

Chalet sites have been developed in all but four of the twenty-six counties. Some could be considered highly successful. Others, unfortunately, could not.

Various factors can militate against the success of a chalet-site, and I think they are worth noting.

1. Built, naturally, of less durable materials than a standard house, the chalet will not stand up to as much wear and tear, and consequently loses its fresh and pretty appearance more quickly—especially where there are numbers of children. Constant supervision and maintenance is required—but not always provided—on the part of the Local Authority, if the families are to be expected to take a pride in their chalets, and to do their share of looking after them.

2. Ill-advised grouping of the families chosen to live together on the site can cause difficulties. It is vitally important that, in this their first introduction to settled living, the families concerned should be known to be congenial to one another. Deep-seated, tribal feuds have often been the cause of serious disturbances, which have brought about the departure of one or more families from the site and a return to the roads.

3. Lack of after-care on the part of the Committee or Social Worker often leaves the chalet families feeling dispirited and neglected. Usually, during the preliminary situation, when those settled individuals were campaigning for sites and shelters for the Travellers, they would have been constant visitors to the camps; and the Travellers would have grown to look forward to their visits and moral support. Once they are settled, if that support is withdrawn, the Travellers feel despondent. They feel they have been "dumped" on the site, merely to get rid of a nuisance, and that no one now seems to care how they live. This is very damaging to their newly-found pride in their new environment.

4. Lack of a regular rent collection is also a cause of discouragement. The payment of rent—no

matter how small—is an important factor in successful settlement. Paradoxically, although the Travellers may find it quite difficult to set aside the money for a weekly rent, yet the paying of it gives them a sense of responsibility and self-respect. It also helps them to value their new homes. Some Local Authorities have been lax in maintaining this regular rent collection on the sites, and it is a pity.

To sum up, then, the most successful chalet sites are those where the families are congenial to one another; where a Local Authority caretaker is employed to supervise the cleanliness and mainte-nance of the site and the chalets; where the families are visited regularly—but not dominated or imposed upon—by a Social Worker and individual voluntary workers, who are known and well-liked by them; and where rents are collected regularly. Further aids to success are provided in sites like those in St Helena's Park, Dundalk, or Milltown Grove, Shinrone, Co. Tipperary. Here we find the addition of Community Centres on the sites, where all kinds of social and cultural activities are provided by voluntary workers for the families, to help them to learn the ways of settled living. Classes in cookery, dressmaking, baby-care, etc. are provided for the women and girls; extra education for the education-ally deprived, and pre-school play-groups for the toddlers; social activities for all. It is interesting to note that the situation on the Milltown Park Chalet Site is so happy and orderly that a family from the settled community has applied for, and been allo-cated, a home among the Travellers.

Trailers on authorised sites

There are about 150 families now living in trailers on serviced sites, officially provided by the Local

Authorities in the area. Those of us who are working with the Travellers are not usually very enthusiastic about these trailer sites, but at least they are an improvement on a roadside camp. They are a god-send, of course, to the families in my third category, i.e. those who would like the security of a legal, settled place to live, without having to commit themselves to the daunting prospect of going into a house. Unfortunately, however, there are far too many families who really want houses, living on these trailer sites.

Trailer sites are usually developed by Local Authorities merely as a stop-gap to get the families off the roads. To give the authorities their due, I do not imagine for a moment that they intend these sites to be any more than a temporary arrangement prior to housing. Unfortunately, in many cases, their good intentions to provide better and more permanent accommodation peter out, and the families are left, in deteriorating trailers, for indefinite periods. One Galway family I know—a man and his wife and twelve children—have been left in the self-same trailer for six years, waiting to be housed.

The appearance of many of these sad-looking trailer sites must be familiar to most of us by now —a group of dilapidated holiday trailers, parked permanently on a tarmacadam surface, with perhaps one tap to serve them all. Those of us who have ever spent a fortnight's holiday in a trailer will know how flimsy and easily-damaged they can be—especi-ally when there are children about. Yet there are people who criticise the Travellers, living in them for years, because they cannot keep them in good condition!

Why then have trailer sites at all? I think the only answer to that is that in many cases where families have been living in appalling conditions on the roadsides, and where they have been constantly harassed and moved on by the authorities, the provision of a trailer on an authorised site has been the only solution. And these sites could, in fact, serve their purpose if certain conditions were maintained on them. If, for instance, the trailers were maintained in good condition, and replaced when they became obsolete; if large families were given a second trailer to live in, to avoid overcrowding; if refuse collections were established at the very start; if the rent for the trailers were collected weekly; if the Local Authority maintained a regular supervision and interest in the site and the families; and lastly, if the families who were waiting there for chalets or standard houses, were not kept waiting too long.

Unfortunately, these conditions have in few cases up to now been fully understood or met by Local Authorities. Consequently, the trailer site has seldom been used in the right way, or served the purpose it was intended to serve.

Halts

In the 1963 Report of the Government Commission on Itinerancy, it was recommended that "Local Authorities should provide halting-places in or near the outskirts of towns and villages which itinerant families at present habitually visit and in which they stay for short periods".

It was realised at that time that the process of housing the Travellers would be slow because of the difficulties involved, and that anyway there would be many families who would be reluctant for quite some time to give up their wandering way of life. These are the families who fall into the fourth and last category I mentioned. I think it is important that those of us who are working with the Travellers do not allow sentimentality or paternalism to blind us to the fact that this last category does exist and is quite a sizable one—perhaps about ten per cent of the total.

These families are just not interested in the idea of a permanent dwelling. It may be simply that they like the wandering life or that the business they are engaged in—scrap dealing, trading in antiques or whatever—demands that they keep on the move. They may not like to feel tied to one place, or they may feel that they can make a better living on the road. Whatever their reasons are, the decision to remain mobile is theirs and must be respected, provided they do not infringe on the rights of other people.

This last proviso, concerning the rights of other people, raises problems which relate to the education of their children, the legality of some of their trading practices, the possibility of trespassing on property or causing obstruction to traffic, etc. But these are separate issues, and must be dealt with by the appropriate authorities. The important point is that they should not, and indeed cannot, be forced to settle against their will. Consequently, it was stated in the Government Report, "there is no charitable or humanitarian alternative to providing at least a place where the itinerant can halt his caravan". The inhumanity of the long-established policy of simply "moving them on" was pin-pointed. It was hoped that it would not be long before the authorities began to realise the necessity for providing halting-places for these really transient travelling people.

Unfortunately this idea has never really been accepted or followed through. To the best of my knowledge, there are only three such halts in the entire country. This is understandable, in view of the difficulties experienced by the Local Authorities in obtaining or allocating land to be used for the Travellers. When they do succeed in earmarking a site for this purpose, they are obviously more liable

to build houses or chalets on it than to provide a
halt for the transient families.

It is understandable, but not very far-seeing. For
while housing may be a priority for the very large
number of families who need it, no matter how
quickly the authorities proceed with their settlement
programme, it will be many years before all the
travelling people are off the roads. Some may never
settle; and in the meantime, these transients will continue to search the countryside for somewhere to park
their caravans. If no legal, authorised halts are provided, they will continue to park in unsuitable places
and cause annoyance to the settled population as well
as hardship to themselves.

To add to that, their continued presence on the
roads will militate against the settlement and integration of others. For as long as the transients continue to have no place where they may legally park
their caravans, they cannot be expected to adopt a
responsible attitude in matters like choosing a suitable site for themselves, and keeping it clean and
tidy. Naturally, this will antagonise the settled
population and confuse the whole issue concerning
the settlement of the others.

A halt has been envisaged as a site to be provided by the Local Authority in or near every
reasonably-sized town or village. It would need to
have hard-standing for caravans, a satisfactory water
supply and sanitary facilities, and a tethering place
for animals. It could be large or small, according to
the needs of the area. Places where it is known that
large numbers of families traditionally gather from
time to time would obviously need a fairly large site
or perhaps more than one; others would only require
space enough for a few caravans. Small demarcation
walls to section off the required number of stands
would avoid over-crowding—a very natural fear on

the part of Local Authorities when considering the development of halts up to now.

In order to maintain order and cleanliness on the halt, official supervision would be needed and a regular refuse collection provided. A small parking fee should be charged as experience has shown that the Travellers are not reluctant to pay for facilities of this kind, and it helps greatly to give them a sense of self-respect and responsibility.

From a Local Authority point of view, the provision and maintenance of a halt is not easy. But it must be agreed surely that coping with the problems of random parking, trespass and obstruction up to now has not been easy either. The provision of a network of halts throughout the various counties would, I feel, greatly alleviate these problems.

Conclusion

These, then, are the various kinds of settlement being provided for the Travellers throughout Ireland. No one method—whether house, chalet, trailer or halt—has been proved decisively the best. All have their advantages and disadvantages. Some families have chosen, and been given, what is right for them; some have not. There have been successes and failures.

The overall pattern, however, is encouraging. Not alone have the hardships of the travelling way of life been alleviated for a great number of families, but a greater spirit of tolerance and understanding is steadily growing amongst the settled community. Prejudice is declining, and with it, the equally nauseating sentimentality adopted by some people. The Travellers are at last being accorded their rights, and are being given the opportunity to help themselves. Most of them are only too anxious to avail of this opportunity.

However, it is safe to say that no matter what efforts are made on their behalf, and no matter how many families become integrated into the settled community, the travelling people will be with us for a very long time to come—even if, or when, the last family ceases to travel. What does the future hold for them? How long will they retain their own identity as a group? What have we, the settled community, to offer them if eventually they become part of us? These are the questions which will confront us, and them, as the years go by.

But even now, with so little accomplished and so much further to go, there is cause for optimism in the fact that at least we are making some small steps forward.

Indeed, it was well summed up in the words of a travelling friend of mine, on the morning after she and her family slept under a roof for the first time : "Well, do you know—it's a miracle."

JOYCE SHOLDICE *was born in 1921 in Co Tipperary. She graduated from Trinity College with an Honours Degree in Modern Languages in 1942. Married, with two sons, she moved to Galway in 1962 and it was there that she first became involved with the Travelling People. She was one of the founder-members of the Galway Itinerant Settlement Committee in 1967. For six years she acted as Hon. Secretary until her present appointment as National Coordinator for Itinerant Settlement.*

How you can help

It is the responsibility of the Local Authority to provide accommodation for the Travellers whether it be houses, serviced sites or halts. Too often this is prevented by opposition. The Local Authority needs the support of public opinion for making the above provision. Make your support known to your Local Authority, either direct, or better still through your Residents' Association if you belong to one. Try to win the support of others by talking to them, by reading any of the following and passing them on to others to read :

Report of Government Commission on Itinerancy obtainable from Government Publications Office, G.P.O. Arcade, Dublin 1. Or this book—obtainable from Veritas Co. Ltd., 7/8 Lower Abbey Street, Dublin 1.

Support those in your district in their efforts to help itinerants. There are settlement committees in most counties. If you don't know the name and address of the secretary of your local committee, write and ask for it from Rev. G. T. Fehily, 31 Herbert Avenue, Dublin 4.

* Make a friendly contact with Travellers as opportunity offers.
* Can you assist in helping Travellers, who want it, to obtain employment?
* Could you offer land for a single family to settle on, or a larger site for a number of families? Or could you encourage someone else to do this?

* Can you help Travellers who need it to get land which they can rent for grazing their animals?

* Have you a skill or craft which would be useful to Travellers that you would be willing to teach them, or do you know anyone else who might do so? Any craft which would enable them to earn a living without having to go into routine employment would be specially valuable.

* Do you belong to a games club or social club which you could encourage Travellers to join, and so help integration?

* Most important of all, talk to people and help to create a favourable public opinion.